Middle Ages
Ages
Biographies

Middle
Ages
Biographies

Volume 1:
A-I

JUDSON KNIGHT
Edited by Judy Galens

N IMPRINT OF THE GALE GROUP
ROIT · NEW YORK · SAN FRANCISCO
LONDON · BOSTON · WOODBRIDGE, CT

Judson Knight

Judy Galens, *Editor*

Staff

Diane Sawinski, *U•X•L Senior Editor*
Carol DeKane Nagel, *U•X•L Managing Editor*
Thomas L. Romig, *U•X•L Publisher*

Margaret Chamberlain, *Permissions Associate (Pictures)*
Maria Franklin, *Permissions Manager*

Randy Bassett, *Imaging Database Supervisor*
Daniel Newell, *Imaging Specialist*
Pamela A. Reed, *Image Coordinator*
Robyn V. Young, *Senior Image Editor*

Rita Wimberley, *Senior Buyer*
Evi Seoud, *Assistant Production Manager*
Dorothy Maki, *Manufacturing Manager*

Pamela A. E. Galbreath, *Senior Art Director*
Kenn Zorn, *Product Design Manager*

Marco Di Vita, the Graphix Group, *Typesetting*

Cover photograph of T'ai Tsung reproduced by permission of the Granger Collection, New York.

Library of Congress Cataloging-in-Publication Data

Knight, Judson.
    Middle ages. Biographies / Judson Knight ; Judy Galens, editor.
      p. cm.
      Includes bibliographical references and index.
    ISBN 0-7876-4857-4 (set) — ISBN 0-7876-4858-2 (vol. 1) — ISBN
      0-7876-4859-0 (vol. 2 : hardcover)
    1. Biography—Middle Ages, 500-1500. 2. Civilization, Medieval. 3.
      World history. I. Galens, Judy, 1968- II. Title.
CT114 .K65 2000
920'.009'02—dc21

00–064864

Printed in the United States of America
10 9 8 7 6 5 4 3 2

Contents

Volume 1 (A–I)

Volume 2 (J–Z)

Reader's Guide

The Middle Ages was an era of great changes in civilization, a transition between ancient times and the modern world. Lasting roughly from A.D. 500 to 1500, the period saw the growth of the Roman Catholic Church in Western Europe and the spread of the Islamic faith in the Middle East. Around the world, empires—the Byzantine, Mongol, and Incan—rose and fell, and the first nation-states emerged in France, England, and Spain. Despite the beauty of illuminated manuscripts, soaring Gothic cathedrals, and the literary classics of Augustine and Dante, Europe's civilization lagged far behind that of the technologically advanced, administratively organized, and economically wealthy realms of the Arab world, West Africa, India, and China.

Middle Ages: Biographies (two volumes) presents the life stories of fifty people who lived during the Middle Ages. Included are such major rulers as Charlemagne, Genghis Khan, and Eleanor of Aquitaine; thinkers and writers Augustine and Thomas Aquinas; religious leaders Muhammad and Francis of Assisi; and great explorers Marco Polo and Leif Eriksson. Also featured are lesser-known figures from the era, including Wu Ze-tian and Irene of Athens, the only female rulers in the history of China and Byzantium, respectively; Mansa Musa, leader of the great empire of Mali in Africa; Japanese woman author Murasaki Shikibu, who penned the world's first novel; and Pachacutec, Inca emperor recognized as among the greatest rulers in history.

Additional features

Over one hundred illustrations and dozens of sidebar boxes exploring high-interest people and topics bring the text to life. Definitions of unfamiliar terms and a list of books and Web sites to consult for more information are included in each entry. The volume also contains a timeline of events, a general glossary, and an index offering easy access to the people, places, and subjects discussed throughout *Middle Ages: Biographies*.

Dedication

To Margaret, my mother; to Deidre, my wife; and to Tyler, my daughter.

Comments and suggestions

We welcome your comments on this work as well as your suggestions for topics to be featured in future editions of *Middle Ages: Biographies*. Please write: Editors, *Middle Ages: Biographies*, U•X•L, 27500 Drake Rd., Farmington Hills, MI 48331-3535; call toll-free: 1-800-877-4253; fax: 248-699-8097; or send e-mail via www.galegroup.com.

Timeline of Events in the Middle Ages

180 The death of Roman emperor Marcus Aurelius marks the end of the "Pax Romana," or Roman peace. Years of instability follow, and although Rome recovers numerous times, this is the beginning of Rome's three-century decline.

312 Roman emperor Constantine converts to Christianity. As a result, the empire that once persecuted Christians will embrace their religion and eventually will begin to persecute other religions.

325 Constantine calls the Council of Nicaea, first of many ecumenical councils at which gatherings of bishops determine official church policy.

330 Constantine establishes Byzantium as eastern capital of the Roman Empire.

395 After the death of Emperor Theodosius, the Roman Empire is permanently divided in half. As time passes, the Eastern Roman Empire (later known as the Byzantine Empire) distances itself from the declining Western Roman Empire.

410 Led by Alaric, the Visigoths sack Rome, dealing the Western Roman Empire a blow from which it will never recover.

413–425 Deeply affected—as are most Roman citizens—by the Visigoths' attack on Rome, **Augustine** writes *City of God*, one of the most important books of the Middle Ages.

455 The Vandals sack Rome.

c. 459 Death of **St. Patrick,** missionary who converted Ireland to Christianity.

476 The German leader Odoacer removes Emperor Romulus Augustulus and crowns himself "king of Italy." This incident marks the end of the Western Roman Empire.

481 The Merovingian Age, named for the only powerful dynasty in Western Europe during the period, begins when **Clovis** takes the throne in France.

496 **Clovis** converts to Christianity. By establishing strong ties with the pope, he forges a strong church-state relationship that will continue throughout the medieval period.

500 Date commonly cited as beginning of Middle Ages.

500–1000 Era in European history often referred to as the Dark Ages, or Early Middle Ages.

524 The philosopher **Boethius,** from the last generation of classically educated Romans, dies in jail, probably at the orders of the Ostrogoth chieftain Theodoric.

529 Benedict of Nursia and his followers establish the monastery at Monte Cassino, Italy. This marks the beginning of the monastic tradition in Europe.

532 Thanks in large part to the counsel of his wife Theodora, **Justinian**—greatest of Byzantine emperors—takes a strong stand in the Nika Revolt, ensuring his continued power.

534–563 Belisarius and other generals under orders from **Justinian** recapture much of the Western Roman Empire, including parts of Italy, Spain, and North Africa. The victories are costly, however, and soon after Justinian's death these lands will fall back into the hands of barbarian tribes such as the Vandals and Lombards.

535 **Justinian** establishes his legal code, a model for the laws in many Western nations today.

540 The Huns, or Hunas, destroy India's Gupta Empire, plunging much of the subcontinent into a state of anarchy.

c. 550 Death of Indian mathematician **Aryabhata**, one of the first mathematicians to use the numeral zero.

589 The ruthless **Wen Ti** places all of China under the rule of his Sui dynasty, ending more than three centuries of upheaval.

590 Pope **Gregory I** begins his fourteen-year reign. Also known as Gregory the Great, he ensures the survival of the church, and becomes one of its greatest medieval leaders.

Late 500s The first Turks begin moving westward, toward the Middle East, from their homeland to the north and west of China.

604 Prince **Shotoku Taishi** of Japan issues his "Seventeen-Article Constitution."

c. 610 An Arab merchant named **Muhammad** receives the first of some 650 revelations that form the basis of the Koran, Islam's holy book.

618 In China, **T'ai Tsung** and his father Kao Tsu overthrow the cruel Sui dynasty, establishing the highly powerful and efficient T'ang dynasty.

622 **Muhammad** and his followers escape the city of Mecca. This event, known as the *hegira,* marks the beginning of the Muslim calendar.

632–661 Following the death of **Muhammad,** the Arab Muslims are led by a series of four caliphs who greatly expand Muslim territories to include most of the Middle East.

645 A conspiracy to murder the Japanese emperor places the reform-minded Emperor Tenchi on the throne and puts the Fujiwara clan—destined to remain influential for centuries—in a position of power.

661	The fifth caliph, Mu'awiya, founds the Umayyad caliphate, which will rule the Muslim world from Damascus, Syria, until 750.
690	**Wu Ze-tian** becomes sole empress of China. She will reign until 705, the only female ruler in four thousand years of Chinese history.
711	Moors from North Africa invade Spain, taking over from the Visigoths. Muslims will rule parts of the Iberian Peninsula until 1492.
711	Arabs invade the Sind in western India, establishing a Muslim foothold on the Indian subcontinent.
727	In Greece, the Iconoclasts begin a sixty-year war on icons, or images of saints and other religious figures, which they consider idols. Though the Greek Orthodox Church ultimately rejects iconoclasm, the controversy helps widen a growing division between Eastern and Western Christianity.
731	**The Venerable Bede** publishes his *Ecclesiastical History of the English People,* his most important work.
732	A force led by Charles Martel repels Moorish invaders at Tours, halting Islam's advance into Western Europe.
750	A descendant of **Muhammad**'s uncle Abbas begins killing off all the Umayyad leaders and establishes the Abbasid caliphate in Baghdad, Iraq.
751	The Carolingian Age begins when Charles Martel's son Pepin III, with the support of the pope, removes the last Merovingian king from power.
751	Defeated by Arab armies at Talas, China's T'ang dynasty begins to decline. A revolt led by An Lu-shan in 755 adds to its troubles.
768	Reign of **Charlemagne**, greatest ruler of Western Europe during the Early Middle Ages, begins.
782	English scholar **Alcuin** goes to France, on the invitation of **Charlemagne**, to organize a school for future officials in the Carolingian empire.
787	**Irene of Athens** convenes the Seventh Council of Nicaea, which restores the use of icons in worship.

793	Viking raiders destroy the church at Lindisfarne off the coast of England. Lindisfarne was one of the places where civilized learning had weathered the darkest years of the Middle Ages. Thus begins two centuries of terror as more invaders pour out of Scandinavia and spread throughout Europe.
797	Having murdered her son, **Irene of Athens**—who actually ruled from 780 onward—officially becomes Byzantine empress, the only woman ruler in the empire's eleven-hundred-year history. It is partly in reaction to Irene that the pope later crowns **Charlemagne** emperor of Western Europe.
800s	Feudalism takes shape in Western Europe.
800	Pope Leo III crowns **Charlemagne** "Emperor of All the Romans." This marks the beginning of the political alliance later to take shape under **Otto the Great** as the Holy Roman Empire.
c. 800	The Khmers, or Cambodians, adopt Hinduism under the leadership of their first powerful king, Jayavarman II, founder of the Angkor Empire.
801	Death of **Rabia al-Adawiyya**, a woman and former slave who founded the mystic Sufi sect of Islam.
820	A group of Vikings settles in northwestern France, where they will become known as Normans.
843	In the Treaty of Verdun, **Charlemagne**'s son Louis the Pious divides the Carolingian Empire among his three sons. These three parts come to be known as the West Frankish Empire, consisting chiefly of modern France; the "Middle Kingdom," a strip running from what is now the Netherlands all the way down to Italy; and the East Frankish Empire, or modern Germany. The Middle Kingdom soon dissolves into a patchwork of tiny principalities.
c. 850	Death of Arab mathematician **al-Khwarizmi**, who coined the term "algebra" and who is often considered the greatest mathematician of the Middle Ages.
860	Vikings discover Iceland.

863	St. Cyril and St. Methodius, two Greek priests, become missionaries to the Slavs of Central and Eastern Europe. As a result, the Greek Orthodox version of Christianity spreads throughout the region, along with the Cyrillic alphabet, which the brothers create in order to translate the Bible into local languages.
886	King Alfred the Great captures London from the Danes, and for the first time in British history unites all Anglo-Saxons.
907	China's T'ang dynasty comes to an end after almost three centuries of rule, and the empire enters a period of instability known as "Five Dynasties and Ten Kingdoms."
911	The last of the Carolingian line in the East Frankish Empire dies. Seven years later, Henry the Fowler of Saxony, father of Otto the Great, takes leadership of the German states.
c. 930	Arab physician al-Razi writes his most important work, *The Comprehensive Book,* which sums up the medical knowledge of the era.
955	German king Otto I defeats a tribe of nomadic invaders called the Magyars. The Magyars later become Christianized and found the nation of Hungary; as for Otto, thenceforth he is known as Otto the Great.
957	Death of al-Mas'udi, perhaps the greatest historian of the Arab world.
960	In China, troops loyal to Chao K'uang-yin declare him emperor, initiating the Sung dynasty.
962	Having conquered most of Central Europe, Otto the Great is crowned emperor in Rome, reviving Charlemagne's title. From this point on, most German kings are also crowned ruler of the Holy Roman Empire.
982	Vikings discover Greenland. Four years later, Erik the Red founds a permanent settlement there.
987	Russia converts to Greek Orthodox Christianity and gradually begins adopting Byzantine culture after Vladimir the Great marries Anne, sister of Emperor Basil II.

987   The last Carolingian ruler of France dies without an heir, and Hugh Capet takes the throne, establishing a dynasty that will last until 1328.

1000–1300 Era in European history often referred to as the High Middle Ages.

1001   Vikings led by **Leif Eriksson** sail westward to North America, and during the next two decades conduct a number of raids on the coast of what is now Canada.

1001   A second Muslim invasion of the Indian subcontinent, this time by Turks, takes place as the Ghaznavids subdue a large region in what is now Afghanistan, Pakistan, and western India.

1002   Holy Roman Emperor **Otto III** dies at the age of twenty-two, and with him die his grand dreams of a revived Roman Empire.

1002   In Japan, **Murasaki Shikibu** begins writing the *Tale of Genji,* the world's first novel.

1014   After years of conflict with the Bulgarians, Byzantine Emperor **Basil II** defeats them. He orders that ninety-nine of every one hundred men be blinded and the last man allowed to keep just one eye so he can lead the others home. Bulgaria's Czar Samuel dies of a heart attack when he sees his men, and Basil earns the nickname "Bulgar-Slayer."

1025   **Basil II** dies, having taken the Byzantine Empire to its greatest height since **Justinian** five centuries earlier; however, it begins a rapid decline soon afterward.

1039   Death of Arab mathematician and physicist **Alhazen,** the first scientist to form an accurate theory of optics, or the mechanics of vision.

1054   After centuries of disagreement over numerous issues, the Greek Orthodox Church and the Roman Catholic Church officially separate.

1060   Five years after Turks seize control of Baghdad from the declining Abbasid caliphate, their leader, Toghril Beg, declares himself sultan and thus establishes the Seljuk dynasty.

1066 **William the Conqueror** leads an invading force that defeats an Anglo-Saxon army at Hastings and wins control of England. The Norman invasion is the most important event of medieval English history, greatly affecting the future of English culture and language.

1071 The Seljuk Turks defeat Byzantine forces at the Battle of Manzikert in Armenia. As a result, the Turks gain a foothold in Asia Minor (today known as Turkey), and the Byzantine Empire begins a long, slow decline.

1071 A Norman warlord named Robert Guiscard drives the last Byzantine forces out of Italy. Byzantium had controlled parts of the peninsula since the time of **Justinian.**

1072 Robert Guiscard's brother Roger expels the Arabs from Sicily, and takes control of the island.

1075–77 Pope **Gregory VII** and Holy Roman Emperor **Henry IV** become embroiled in a church-state struggle called the Investiture Controversy, a debate over whether popes or emperors should have the right to appoint local bishops. Deserted by his supporters, Henry stands barefoot in the snow for three days outside the gates of a castle in Canossa, Italy, waiting to beg the pope's forgiveness.

1084 Reversing the results of an earlier round in the Investiture Controversy, **Henry IV** takes Rome and forcibly removes **Gregory VII** from power. The pope dies soon afterward, broken and humiliated.

1084 **Ssu-ma Kuang**, an official in the Sung dynasty, completes his monumental history of China, *Comprehensive Mirror for Aid in Government.*

1094 Troops under the leadership of Rodrigo Díaz de Vivar—better known as **El Cid**—defeat the Moorish Almoravids at Valencia. This victory, and the character of El Cid himself, becomes a symbol of the Reconquista, the Christian effort to reclaim Spain from its Muslim conquerors.

1094 Norman warrior Bohemond, son of Robert Guiscard, takes control of Rome from **Henry IV** and hands the city over to Pope Urban II. Fearing the Normans' power and aware that he owes them a great debt, Urban looks for something to divert their attention.

1095 Byzantine Emperor Alexis Comnenus asks Urban II for military assistance against the Turks. Urban preaches a sermon to raise support at the Council of Clermont in France, and in the resulting fervor the First Crusade begins. Among its leaders are Bohemond and his nephew Tancred.

1096–97 A pathetic sideshow called the Peasants' Crusade plays out before the real First Crusade gets underway. The peasants begin by robbing and killing thousands of Jews in Germany; then, led by Peter the Hermit, they march toward the Holy Land, wreaking havoc as they go. In Anatolia, a local Turkish sultan leads them into a trap, and most of the peasants are killed.

1099 The First Crusade ends in victory for the Europeans as they conquer Jerusalem. It is a costly victory, however—one in which thousands of innocent Muslims, as well as many Europeans, have been brutally slaughtered—and it sows resentment between Muslims and Christians that remains strong today.

c. 1100–1300 Many of the aspects of life most commonly associated with the Middle Ages, including heraldry and chivalry, make their appearance in Western Europe during this period. Returning crusaders adapt the defensive architecture they observed in fortresses of the Holy Land, resulting in the familiar design of the medieval castle. This is also the era of romantic and heroic tales such as those of King Arthur.

1105 King Henry I of England and St. **Anselm of Canterbury**, head of the English church, sign an agreement settling their differences. This is an important milestone in church-state relations and serves as the model for the Concordat of Worms seventeen years later.

1118 After being banished because of her part in a conspiracy against her brother, the Byzantine emperor, **Anna Comnena** begins writing the *Alexiad*, a history of Byzantium in the period 1069–1118.

1140 After a career in which he infuriated many with his unconventional views on God, French philosopher **Peter Abelard** is charged with heresy by **Bernard of Clairvaux** and forced to publicly refute his beliefs.

c. 1140 In Cambodia, Khmer emperor Suryavarman II develops the splendid temple complex of Angkor Wat.

1146 After the Muslims' capture of Edessa in 1144, Pope Eugenius III calls on the help of his former teacher, **Bernard of Clairvaux**, who makes a speech that leads to the launching of the Second Crusade.

1147–49 In the disastrous Second Crusade, armies from Europe are double-crossed by their crusader allies in the Latin Kingdom of Jerusalem. They fail to recapture Edessa and suffer a heavy defeat at Damascus. Among the people who take part in the crusade (though not as a combatant) is **Eleanor of Aquitaine.**

1154 After the death of England's King Stephen, Henry II takes the throne, beginning the long Plantaganet dynasty. With Henry is his new bride, **Eleanor of Aquitaine.** Now queen of England, she had been queen of France two years earlier, before the annulment of her marriage to King Louis VII.

1158 Holy Roman Emperor **Frederick I Barbarossa** establishes Europe's first university at Bologna, Italy.

1159 **Frederick I Barbarossa** begins a quarter-century of fruitless, costly wars in which the Ghibellines and Guelphs—factions representing pro-imperial and pro-church forces, respectively—fight for control of northern Italy.

1162 **Moses Maimonides**, greatest Jewish philosopher of the Middle Ages, publishes his *Letter Concerning Apostasy,* the first of many important works by him that will appear over the next four decades.

1165 A letter supposedly written by Prester John, a Christian monarch in the East, appears in Europe. Over the centuries that follow, Europeans will search in vain for Prester John, hoping for his aid in their war against Muslim forces. Even as Europe enters the modern era, early proponents of exploration such as

Henry the Navigator will remain inspired by the quest for Prester John's kingdom.

1170 Knights loyal to Henry II murder the archbishop **Thomas à Becket** in his cathedral at Canterbury.

1174–80 Arab philosopher **Averroës** writes one of his most important works, *The Incoherence of the Incoherence,* a response to hard-line Muslim attacks on his belief that reason and religious faith can coexist.

1183 **Frederick I Barbarossa** signs the Peace of Constance with the cities of the Lombard League, and thus ends his long war in northern Italy. After this he will concentrate his attention on Germany and institute reforms that make him a hero in his homeland.

1185 For the first time, Japan comes under the rule of a shogun, or military dictator. Shoguns will remain in power for the next four centuries.

1187 Muslim armies under **Saladin** deal the crusaders a devastating blow at the Battle of Hittin in Palestine. Shortly afterward, Saladin leads his armies in the reconquest of Jerusalem.

1189 In response to **Saladin**'s victories, Europeans launch the Third Crusade. Of the crusade's three principal leaders, Emperor **Frederick I Barbarossa** drowns on his way to the Holy Land, and **Richard** I takes a number of detours, only arriving in 1191. This leaves Philip II Augustus of France to fight the Muslims alone.

1191 Led by **Richard** I of England and Philip II of France, crusaders take the city of Acre in Palestine.

1192 **Richard** I signs a treaty with **Saladin**, ending the Third Crusade.

1198 Pope **Innocent III** begins an eighteen-year reign that marks the high point of the church's power. Despite his great influence, however, when he calls for a new crusade to the Holy Land, he gets little response—a sign that the spirit behind the Crusades is dying.

c. 1200 Cambodia's Khmer Empire reaches its height under Jayavarman VII.

1202 Four years after the initial plea from the pope, the Fourth Crusade begins. Instead of going to the Holy Land, however, the crusaders become involved in a power struggle for the Byzantine throne.

1204 Acting on orders from the powerful city-state of Venice, crusaders take Constantinople, forcing the Byzantines to retreat to Trebizond in Turkey. The Fourth Crusade ends with the establishment of the Latin Empire.

1206 Qutb-ud-Din Aybak, the first independent Muslim ruler in India, establishes the Delhi Sultanate.

1206 **Genghis Khan** unites the Mongols for the first time in their history and soon afterward leads them to war against the Sung dynasty in China.

1208 Pope **Innocent III** launches the Albigensian Crusade against the Cathars, a heretical sect in southern France.

1209 **St. Francis of Assisi** establishes the Franciscan order.

1215 In Rome, Pope **Innocent III** convenes the Fourth Lateran Council. A number of traditions, such as regular confession of sin to a priest, are established at this, one of the most significant ecumenical councils in history.

1215 English noblemen force King John to sign the Magna Carta, which grants much greater power to the nobility. Ultimately the agreement will lead to increased freedom for the people from the power of both king and nobles.

1217–21 In the Fifth Crusade, armies from England, Germany, Hungary, and Austria attempt unsuccessfully to conquer Egypt.

1227 **Genghis Khan** dies, having conquered much of China and Central Asia, thus laying the foundation for the largest empire in history.

1228–29 The Sixth Crusade, led by Holy Roman Emperor **Frederick II**, results in a treaty that briefly restores Christian control of Jerusalem—and does so with a minimum of bloodshed.

1229   The brutal Albigensian Crusade ends. Not only are the Cathars destroyed, but so is much of the French nobility, thus greatly strengthening the power of the French king.

1231   Pope Gregory IX establishes the Inquisition, a court through which the church will investigate, try, and punish cases of heresy.

c. 1235 The empire of Mali, most powerful realm in sub-Saharan Africa at the time, takes shape under the leadership of Sundiata Keita.

1239–40 In the Seventh Crusade, Europeans make another failed attempt to retake the Holy Land.

1241   After six years of campaigns in which they sliced across Russia and Eastern Europe, a Mongol force is poised to take Vienna, Austria, and thus to swarm into Western Europe. But when their leader, Batu Khan, learns that the Great Khan Ogodai is dead, he rushes back to the Mongol capital at Karakorum to participate in choosing a successor.

1242   **Alexander Nevsky** and his brother Andrew lead the Russians' defense of Novgorod against invaders from Germany.

1243   Back on the warpath, but this time in the Middle East, the Mongols defeat the last remnants of the Seljuk Turks.

1248–54 King Louis IX of France (St. Louis) leads the Eighth Crusade, this time against the Mamluks. The result is the same: yet another defeat for the Europeans.

1252   In Egypt, a group of former slave soldiers called the Mamluks take power from the Ayyubid dynasty, established many years before by **Saladin.**

1260   The Mamluks become the first force to defeat the Mongols, in a battle at Goliath Spring in Palestine.

1260   **Kublai Khan,** greatest Mongol leader after his grandfather **Genghis Khan,** is declared Great Khan, or leader of the Mongols.

1261   Led by Michael VIII Palaeologus, the Byzantines recapture Constantinople from the Latin Empire, and

Byzantium enjoys one last gasp of power before it goes into terminal decline.

1270–72 In the Ninth Crusade, last of the numbered crusades, King Louis IX of France again leads the Europeans against the Mamluks, who defeat European forces yet again.

1271 **Marco Polo** embarks on his celebrated journey to the East, which lasts twenty-four years.

1273 The Hapsburg dynasty—destined to remain a major factor in European politics until 1918—takes control of the Holy Roman Empire.

1273 Italian philosopher and theologian **Thomas Aquinas** completes the crowning work of his career, the monumental *Summa theologica*. The influential book will help lead to wider acceptance of the idea, introduced earlier by **Moses Maimonides**, **Averroës**, and **Abelard**, that reason and faith are compatible.

1279 Mongol forces under **Kublai Khan** win final victory over China's Sung dynasty. Thus begins the Yüan dynasty, the first time in Chinese history when the country has been ruled by foreigners.

1291 Mamluks conquer the last Christian stronghold at Acre, bringing to an end two centuries of crusades to conquer the Holy Land for Christendom.

1292 Death of **Roger Bacon**, one of Europe's most important scientists. His work helped to show the rebirth of scientific curiosity taking place in Europe as a result of contact with the Arab world during the Crusades.

1294 At the death of **Kublai Khan**, the Mongol realm is the largest empire in history, covering most of Asia and a large part of Europe. Within less than a century, however, this vast empire will have all but disappeared.

1299 Turkish chieftain **Osman I** refuses to pay tribute to the local Mongol rulers, marking the beginnings of the Ottoman Empire.

1300–1500 Era in European history often referred to as the Late Middle Ages.

1303   After years of conflict with Pope Boniface VIII, France's King Philip the Fair briefly has the pope arrested. This event and its aftermath marks the low point of the papacy during the Middle Ages.

1308   **Dante Alighieri** begins writing the *Divine Comedy,* which he will complete shortly before his death in 1321.

1309   Pope Clement V, an ally of Philip the Fair, moves the papal seat from Rome to Avignon in southern France.

1309   After years of fighting, Sultan **Ala-ud-din Muhammad Khalji** subdues most of India.

1324   **Mansa Musa**, emperor of Mali, embarks on a pilgrimage to Mecca. After stopping in Cairo, Egypt, and spending so much gold that he affects the region's economy for years, he becomes famous throughout the Western world: the first sub-Saharan African ruler widely known among Europeans.

1328   Because of a dispute between the Franciscans and the papacy, **William of Ockham**, one of the late medieval period's most important philosophers, is forced to flee the papal court. He remains under the protection of the Holy Roman emperor for the rest of his life.

1337   England and France begin fighting what will become known as the Hundred Years' War, an on-again, off-again struggle to control parts of France.

1347–51   Europe experiences one of the worst disasters in human history, an epidemic called the Black Death. Sometimes called simply "the Plague," in four years the Black Death kills some thirty-five million people, or approximately one-third of the European population in 1300.

1368   Led by Chu Yüan-chang, a group of rebels overthrows the Mongol Yüan dynasty of China and establishes the Ming dynasty, China's last native-born ruling house.

1378   The Catholic Church becomes embroiled in the Great Schism, which will last until 1417. During this time, there are rival popes in Rome and Avignon; and from 1409 to 1417, there is even a third pope in Pisa, Italy.

1383 **Tamerlane** embarks on two decades of conquest in which he strikes devastating blows against empires in Turkey, Russia, and India and subdues a large portion of central and southwestern Asia.

1386 **Geoffrey Chaucer** begins writing the *Canterbury Tales.*

1389 Ottoman forces defeat the Serbs in battle at Kosovo Field. As a result, all of Southeastern Europe except for Greece falls under Turkish control.

1390 **Tamerlane** attacks and severely weakens the Golden Horde even though its leaders come from the same Mongol and Tatar ancestry as he.

1392 General Yi Song-ye seizes power in Korea and establishes a dynasty that will remain in control until 1910.

1398 **Tamerlane** sacks the Indian city of Delhi, hastening the end of the Delhi Sultanate, which comes in 1413.

1402 After conquering much of Iran and surrounding areas and then moving westward, **Tamerlane** defeats the Ottoman sultan Bajazed in battle. An unexpected result of their defeat is that the Ottomans, who seemed poised to take over much of Europe, go into a period of decline.

1404–05 **Christine de Pisan**, Europe's first female professional writer, publishes *The Book of the City of Ladies,* her most celebrated work.

1405 Ming dynasty emperor Yung-lo sends Admiral Cheng Ho on the first of seven westward voyages. These take place over the next quarter-century, during which time Chinese ships travel as far as East Africa.

1417 The Council of Constance ends the Great Schism, affirming that Rome is the seat of the church and that Pope Martin V is its sole leader. Unfortunately for the church, the Great Schism has weakened it at the very time that it faces its greatest challenge ever: a gathering movement that will come to be known as the Reformation.

1418   The "school" of navigation founded by Prince **Henry the Navigator** sponsors the first of many expeditions that, over the next forty-two years, will greatly increase knowledge of the middle Atlantic Ocean and Africa's west coast. These are the earliest European voyages of exploration, of which there will be many in the next two centuries.

1421   Emperor Yung-lo moves the Chinese capital from Nanjing to Beijing, where it has remained virtually ever since.

1429   A tiny French army led by **Joan of Arc** forces the English to lift their siege on the town of Orléans, a victory that raises French spirits and makes it possible for France's king Charles VII to be crowned later that year. This marks a turning point in the Hundred Years' War.

1430–31 Captured by Burgundian forces, **Joan of Arc** is handed over to the English, who arrange her trial for witchcraft in a court of French priests. The trial, a mockery of justice, ends with Joan being burned at the stake.

1431   In Southeast Asia, the Thais conquer the Angkor Empire.

1431   The Aztecs become the dominant partner in a triple alliance with two nearby city-states and soon afterward gain control of the Valley of Mexico.

1438   **Pachacutec Inca Yupanqui**, greatest Inca ruler, takes the throne.

1440   **Montezuma I** takes the Aztec throne.

1441   Fourteen black slaves are brought from Africa to Portugal, where they are presented to Prince **Henry the Navigator.** This is the beginning of the African slave trade, which isn't abolished until more than four centuries later.

1451	The recovery of the Ottoman Empire, which had suffered a half-century of decline, begins under Mehmet the Conqueror.
1453	Due in large part to the victories of **Joan of Arc**, which lifted French morale twenty-four years earlier, the Hundred Years' War ends with French victory.
1453	Turks under Mehmet the Conqueror march into Constantinople, bringing about the fall of the Byzantine Empire. Greece will remain part of the Ottoman Empire until 1829.
1455	Having developed a method of movable-type printing, Johannes Gutenberg of Mainz, Germany, prints his first book: a Bible. In the years to come, the invention of the printing press will prove to be one of the most important events in world history.
1456	A commission directed by Pope Calixtus III declares that the verdict against **Joan of Arc** in 1431 had been wrongfully obtained.
1470	One of the first printed books to appear in England, *La Morte D'Arthur* by Sir Thomas Malory helps establish the now-familiar tales of Arthurian legend.
1492	Spain, united by the 1469 marriage of its two most powerful monarchs, Ferdinand II of Aragon and Isabella I of Castile, drives out the last of the Muslims and expels all Jews. A less significant event of 1492, from the Spanish perspective, is the launch of a naval expedition in search of a westward sea route to China. Its leader is an Italian sailor named Christopher Columbus, who has grown up heavily influenced by **Marco Polo**'s account of his travels.
1493	**Mohammed I Askia** takes the throne of Africa's Songhai Empire, which will reach its height under his leadership.
1500	Date commonly cited as the end of Middle Ages, and the beginning of the Renaissance.
1517	Exactly a century after the Council of Constance ended the Great Schism, a German monk named Martin Luther publicly posts ninety-five theses, or statements challenging the established teachings of

Catholicism, on the door of a church in Germany. Over the next century, numerous new Protestant religious denominations will be established.

1521   Spanish forces led by the conquistador Hernán Cortés destroy the Aztec Empire.

1526   Babur, a descendant of **Tamerlane**, invades India and establishes what becomes the Mogul Empire.

1533   Francisco Pizarro and the Spanish forces with him arrive in Peru and soon bring about the end of the Inca Empire.

1591   Songhai, the last of the great premodern empires in Africa's Sudan region, falls to invaders from Morocco.

1806   In the process of conquering most of Europe, Napoleon Bonaparte brings the Holy Roman Empire to an end.

1912   More than twenty-one centuries of imperial rule in China end with the overthrow of the government by revolutionary forces, who establish a republic.

1918   Among the many outcomes of World War I are the disintegration of several empires with roots in the Middle Ages: the Austro-Hungarian, Ottoman, and Russian empires.

1960s   Nearly a thousand years after **Leif Eriksson** and other Vikings visited the New World, archaeologists find remains of a Norse settlement in Newfoundland.

Words to Know

A

Age of Exploration: The period from about 1450 to about 1750 when European explorers conducted their most significant voyages and travels around the world.

Alchemy: A semi-scientific discipline that holds that through the application of certain chemical processes, ordinary metals can be turned into gold.

Algebra: A type of mathematics used to determine the value of unknown quantities where these can be related to known numbers.

Allegory: A type of narrative, popular throughout the Middle Ages, in which characters represent ideas.

Anarchy: Breakdown of political order.

Ancestor: An earlier person in one's line of parentage, usually more distant in time than a grandparent.

Anti-Semitism: Hatred of, or discrimination against, Jews.

Antipope: A priest proclaimed pope by one group or another, but not officially recognized by the church.

Archaeology: The scientific study of past civilizations.

Archbishop: The leading bishop in an area or nation.

Aristocracy: The richest and most powerful members of society.

Ascetic: A person who renounces all earthly pleasures as part of his or her search for religious understanding.

Assassination: Killing, usually of an important leader, for political reasons.

Astronomy: The scientific study of the stars and other heavenly bodies and their movement in the sky.

B

Barbarian: A negative term used to describe someone as uncivilized.

Bishop: A figure in the Christian church assigned to oversee priests and believers in a given city or region.

Bureaucracy: A network of officials who run a government.

C

Caliph: A successor to Muhammad as spiritual and political leader of Islam.

Caliphate: The domain ruled by a caliph.

Canonization: Formal declaration of a deceased person as a saint.

Cardinal: An office in the Catholic Church higher than that of bishop or archbishop; the seventy cardinals in the "College of Cardinals" participate in electing the pope.

Cavalry: Soldiers on horseback.

Chivalry: The system of medieval knighthood, particularly its code of honor with regard to women.

Christendom: The Christian world.

Church: The entire Christian church, or more specifically the Roman Catholic Church.

City-state: A city that is also a self-contained political unit, like a country.

Civil service: The administrators and officials who run a government.

Civilization: A group of people possessing most or all of the following: a settled way of life, agriculture, a written language, an organized government, and cities.

Classical: Referring to ancient Greece and Rome.

Clergy: The priesthood.

Clerical: Relating to priests.

Coat of arms: A heraldic emblem representing a family or nation.

Commoner: Someone who is not a member of a royal or noble class.

Communion: The Christian ceremony of commemorating the last supper of Jesus Christ.

Courtly love: An idealized form of romantic love, usually of a knight or poet for a noble lady.

D

Dark Ages: A negative term sometimes used to describe the Early Middle Ages, the period from the fall of Rome to about A.D. 1000 in Western Europe.

Deity: A god.

Dialect: A regional variation on a language.

Diplomacy: The use of skillful negotiations with leaders of other nations to influence events.

Duchy: An area ruled by a duke, the highest rank of European noble below a prince.

Dynasty: A group of people, often but not always a family, who continue to hold a position of power over a period of time.

E

Economy: The whole system of production, distribution, and consumption of goods and services in a country.

Ecumenical: Across all faiths, or across all branches of the Christian Church.

Empire: A large political unit that unites many groups of people, often over a wide territory.

Epic: A long poem that recounts the adventures of a legendary hero.

Ethnic group: People who share a common racial, cultural, national, linguistic, or tribal origin.

Excommunicate: To banish someone from the church.

F

Famine: A food shortage caused by crop failures.

Fasting: Deliberately going without food, often but not always for religious reasons.

Feudalism: A form of political and economic organization in which peasants are subject to a noble who owns most or all of the land that they cultivate.

G

Geometry: A type of mathematics dealing with various shapes, their properties, and their measurements.

Guild: An association to promote, and set standards for, a particular profession or business.

H

Hajj: A pilgrimage to Mecca, which is expected of all Muslims who can afford to make it.

Heraldry: The practice of creating and studying coats of arms and other insignia.

Heresy: A belief that goes against established church teachings.

Holy Land: Palestine.

Horde: A division within the Mongol army; the term "hordes" was often used to describe the Mongol armies.

I

Icon: In the Christian church, an image of a saint.

Idol: A statue of a god that the god's followers worship.

Illumination: Decoration of a manuscript with elaborate designs.

Indo-European languages: The languages of Europe, India, Iran, and surrounding areas, which share common roots.

Indulgence: The granting of forgiveness of sins in exchange for an act of service for, or payment to, the church.

Infantry: Foot soldiers.

Infidel: An unbeliever.

Intellectual: A person whose profession or lifestyle centers around study and ideas.

Interest: In economics, a fee charged by a lender against a borrower—usually a percentage of the amount borrowed.

Investiture: The power of a feudal lord to grant lands or offices.

Islam: A religious faith that teaches submission to the one god Allah and his word as given through his prophet Muhammad in the Koran.

J

Jihad: Islamic "holy war" to defend or extend the faith.

K

Khan: A Central Asian chieftain.

Koran: The holy book of Islam.

L

Legal code: A system of laws.

Lingua franca: A common language.

M

Martyr: Someone who willingly dies for his or her faith.

Mass: A Catholic church service.

Medieval: Of or relating to the Middle Ages.

Middle Ages: Roughly the period from A.D. 500 to 1500.

Middle class: A group whose income level falls between that of the rich and the poor, or the rich and the working class; usually considered the backbone of a growing economy.

Millennium: A period of a thousand years.

Missionary: Someone who travels to other lands with the aim of converting others to his or her religion.

Monastery: A place in which monks live.

Monasticism: The tradition and practices of monks.

Monk: A man who leaves the outside world to take religious vows and live in a monastery, practicing a lifestyle of denying earthly pleasures.

Monotheism: Worship of one god.

Mosque: A Muslim temple.

Movable-type printing: An advanced printing process using pre-cast pieces of metal type.

Muezzin: A crier who calls worshipers to prayer five times a day in the Muslim world.

Mysticism: The belief that one can attain direct knowledge of God or ultimate reality through some form of meditation or special insight.

N

Nationalism: A sense of loyalty and devotion to one's nation.

Nation-state: A geographical area composed largely of a single nationality, in which a single national government clearly holds power.

New World: The Americas, or the Western Hemisphere.

Noble: A ruler within a kingdom who has an inherited title and lands but who is less powerful than the king or queen; collectively, nobles are known as the "nobility."

Nomadic: Wandering.

Novel: An extended, usually book-length, work of fiction.

Nun: The female equivalent of a monk, who lives in a nunnery, convent, or abbey.

O

Order: An organized religious community within the Catholic Church.

Ordination: Formal appointment as a priest or minister.

P

Pagan: Worshiping many gods.

Papacy: The office of the pope.

Papal: Referring to the pope.

Patriarch: A bishop in the Eastern Orthodox Church.

Patron: A supporter, particularly of arts, education, or sciences. The term is often used to refer to a ruler or wealthy person who provides economic as well as personal support.

Peasant: A farmer who works a small plot of land.

Penance: An act ordered by the church to obtain forgiveness for sin.

Persecutions: In early church history, Roman punishment of Christians for their faith.

Philosophy: An area of study concerned with subjects including values, meaning, and the nature of reality.

Pilgrimage: A journey to a site of religious significance.

Plague: A disease that spreads quickly to a large population.

Polytheism: Worship of many gods.

Pope: The bishop of Rome, and therefore the head of the Catholic Church.

Principality: An area ruled by a prince, the highest-ranking form of noble below a king.

Prophet: Someone who receives communications directly from God and passes these on to others.

Prose: Written narrative, as opposed to poetry.

Purgatory: A place of punishment after death where, according to Roman Catholic beliefs, a person who has not been damned may work out his or her salvation and earn his or her way to heaven.

R

Rabbi: A Jewish teacher or religious leader.

Racism: The belief that race is the primary factor determining peoples' abilities and that one race is superior to another.

Reason: The use of the mind to figure things out; usually contrasted with emotion, intuition, or faith.

Reformation: A religious movement in the 1500s that ultimately led to the rejection of Roman Catholicism by various groups who adopted Protestant interpretations of Christianity.

Regent: Someone who governs a country when the monarch is too young, too old, or too sick to lead.

Relic: An object associated with the saints of the New Testament or the martyrs of the early church.

Renaissance: A period of renewed interest in learning and the arts that began in Europe during the 1300s and continued to the 1600s.

Representational art: Artwork intended to show a specific subject, whether a human figure, landscape, still life, or a variation on these.

Ritual: A type of religious ceremony that is governed by very specific rules.

Rome: A term sometimes used to refer to the papacy.

S

Sack: To destroy, usually a city.

Saracen: A negative term used in medieval Europe to describe Muslims.

Scientific method: A means of drawing accurate conclusions by collecting information, studying data, and forming theories or hypotheses.

Scriptures: Holy texts.

Sect: A small group within a larger religion.

Secular: Of the world; typically used in contrast to "spiritual."

Semitic: A term describing a number of linguistic and cultural groups in the Middle East, including the modern-day Arabs and Israelis.

Serf: A peasant subject to a feudal system and possessing no land.

Siege: A sustained military attack against a city.

Simony: The practice of buying and selling church offices.

Sultan: A type of king in the Muslim world.

Sultanate: An area ruled by a Sultan.

Synagogue: A Jewish temple.

T

Technology: The application of knowledge to make the performance of physical and mental tasks easier.

Terrorism: Frightening (and usually harming) a group of people in order to achieve a specific political goal.

Theologian: Someone who analyzes religious faith.

Theology: The study of religious faith.

Trial by ordeal: A system of justice in which the accused (and sometimes the accuser as well) has to undergo various physical hardships in order to prove innocence.

Tribal: Describes a society, sometimes nomadic, in which members are organized by families and clans, not by region, and in which leadership comes from warrior-chieftains.

Tribute: Forced payments to a conqueror.

Trigonometry: The mathematical study of triangles, angles, arcs, and their properties and applications.

Trinity: The three persons of God according to Christianity—Father, Son, and Holy Spirit.

U

Usury: Loaning money for a high rate of interest; during the Middle Ages, however, it meant simply loaning money for interest.

V

Vassal: A noble or king who is subject to a more powerful noble or king.

Vatican: The seat of the pope's power in Rome.

W

West: Generally, Western Europe and North America, or the countries influenced both by ancient Greece and ancient Rome.

Working class: A group between the middle class and the poor who typically earn a living with their hands.

Peter Abelard

Born c. 1079
Died 1142

French philosopher

Peter Abelard was a philosopher, meaning that his writings addressed the nature of values and reality. Like most European thinkers of his time, Abelard was particularly concerned with a better understanding of Christianity. This led him into investigations of ethics, or the philosophy of right and wrong. His belief that sin has more to do with a person's attitude than with their actions would hardly raise any eyebrows today, but in twelfth-century France, such ideas nearly got him killed. In a time and place when the authority of the Bible and the Catholic Church were absolute, Abelard seemed to be questioning both. Similarly, his explanations concerning the nature of ideas placed him at odds with many of the leading minds of the day.

But Abelard is not remembered merely as a thinker; his tragic but tender love affair with Héloïse, a student who became his wife and later simply his friend, is a compelling story in its own right. Today the two occupy a place among the ranks of the world's great lovers.

"God considered not action, but the spirit of the action. It is the intention, not the deed, wherein the merit or praise of the doer consists."

Ethics

Fighting with ideas and not swords

Peter Abelard was born in Le Pallet (pah-LAY), a village in the region of Brittany, a peninsula in the northwest part of France. His father, Berengar, was a lord and knight, and his parents expected him to follow in these professions, but from an early age he showed a greater interest in fighting with ideas than in fighting with swords.

In medieval Europe, there was only one place for an intellectual, a person whose profession or lifestyle centers around study and ideas: the church. This meant that he would have to pursue a career in the priesthood, which in turn meant that he could never marry—a fact that would later have a great effect on his life.

At the age of fifteen, Abelard left his parents, his three brothers, and his sister, to study under Roscelin de Compiègne (rawz-LAn duh KAHn-pyan). A priest and philosopher, Roscelin had recently been forced to change his teachings about the Trinity (the Father, Son, and Holy Ghost who make up the three parts of the Christian God) because his claim that they were actually three separate gods went against established beliefs of the church. Like Roscelin, Abelard would later get into a great deal of trouble with his ideas.

"The unconquerable rhinoceros"

In 1100, Abelard went to the French capital of Paris, where he began studying under Guillaume (gee-YOHM), or William, of Champeaux (sham-POH). William was a high official at the Cathedral of Notre Dame (NOH-truh DAHM), the greatest church in France, and therefore a powerful man. Perhaps if young Abelard had been as wise as he was smart, he would not have humiliated William as he did in a public debate concerning the nature of ideas.

Abelard's victory over William won him a number of admirers among his classmates, who dubbed him *Rhinoceros indomitus,* or "the unconquerable rhinoceros." But it made a life-long enemy of William, and by 1102, Abelard had left Notre Dame to establish a school of his own outside the capital. Meanwhile William, no doubt because of his recent shaming by Abelard, left Notre Dame for another appointment as well.

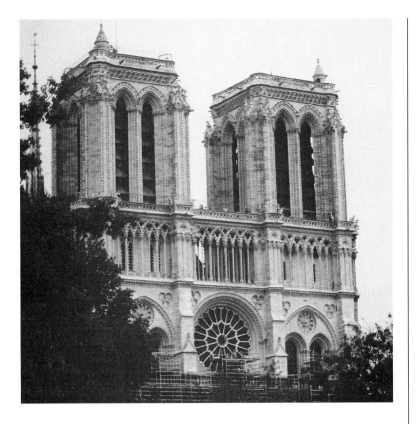

Abelard studied and taught at the Cathedral of Notre Dame in Paris, France.
Reproduced by permission of Daniel L. Gore.

Abelard suffered a brief illness and returned to Brittany, but in 1108 was invited to take William's old job at Notre Dame. This so infuriated William that he returned to Paris and forced Abelard out, whereupon the young scholar began teaching at another school. Most of the students at Notre Dame left the cathedral to study under Abelard, their new hero.

Anselm of Laon

After another brief period at home, in 1113 Abelard went to study with Anselm of Laon (LAH-own; died 1117). Like William before him, Anselm—not to be confused with Anselm of Canterbury (c. 1034–1109), a philosopher regarded by many historians as Abelard's equal—was a highly respected teacher; and as with William, Abelard made a fool of him.

Because Abelard skipped many of Anselm's classes, some of his classmates challenged his lack of respect. Abelard

Li Po

Like Abelard, the Chinese poet Li Po (BOH; 701–762) was a brash, highly talented figure whose recklessness often got him into trouble. Because his ancestors had been exiled to the northern part of China, they had intermarried with the Mongols, a hardy tribal people of that region. As a result, Li Po was taller than most Chinese. He also had different ideas about the world, having been exposed primarily to Taoist (DOW-ist) rather than Confucian teachings. Confucianism, which dominated Chinese thinking, taught submission to people in authority, whereas Taoism urged followers to seek meaning by removing themselves from society.

From his youth, Li Po seemed wild and uncontrollable, and as a young man he associated with ruffians who were fond of sword-fighting. Though he married and had children, he spent much of the time wandering the countryside by himself, and he began writing what many scholars consider some of the finest work composed by a Chinese poet. He also took to excessive drinking; he believed that when he was drunk he had a higher understanding of reality.

At one point Li Po was befriended by the emperor Hsüan Tsung (shwee-AHND-zoong; ruled 712–56), who so admired his work that he once served Li Po food with his own hands—an almost unthinkable act of humility for a Chinese ruler. One of Li Po's most famous poems was "A Song of Pure Happiness," which he wrote in celebration of the emperor's beautiful concubine, Yang Kuei-fei (see box in Irene of Athens entry).

At a later point, however, Li offended a member of the imperial court—perhaps even the emperor himself—and he again wandered the country. During this time, he associated with Tu Fu (doo-FOO; 712–770), a poet whom many critics consider Li Po's equal. Tu Fu had an entirely different approach to life than Li Po, and was a calming influence on him.

During the widespread rebellion led by Yang Kuei-fei's lover, An Lu-shan, which nearly toppled the government of the T'ang dynasty, Li Po was imprisoned. He only gained his release through the help of a soldier he had befriended many years before. He returned to his wife and lived out his days quietly. According to folklore, Li Po died of drowning: supposedly he was drunk in his boat on a beautiful evening, and leaned too far over the side to admire his reflection in the moonlit water.

announced that he could do a better job than his teacher, and to prove it he prepared a lecture of his own. The subject was Ezekiel, one of the most challenging books of the Bible, and Abelard spent a single day in preparation. The next day, he spoke so brilliantly that most of Anselm's students deserted him in favor of Abelard.

Thus Abelard gained a new enemy, and Anselm saw to it that the upstart was forbidden from teaching anywhere in the region. By then, however, William's old job at Notre Dame was vacant once again, and Abelard took it. He could not have suspected that his great pride was about to lead him into misfortune.

Abelard and Héloïse

A handsome man with deep brown eyes, Abelard was a commanding presence. In his style of teaching, he rejected the old method of simply reading a text along with all the established commentaries on it; instead, he favored an active approach, introducing an idea and then grappling with it verbally through careful analysis. This made him an exciting lecturer, and won him countless admirers.

Among these was a high official at Notre Dame named Fulbert (fool-BEHR), who in 1117 invited Abelard to come live with him and tutor his niece Héloïse (EL-oh-eez; c. 1100–1164). Abelard was thirty-eight and Héloïse seventeen—tall, with fine features, a gracious manner, and great intelligence. The outcome of their long hours together should not have come as a surprise to anyone: as Abelard himself recalled, "More words of love than of our reading passed between us, and more kissing than teaching."

Tragedy

By the time Fulbert realized what was going on and ordered Abelard to leave his home, Héloïse was pregnant. Abelard took her with him to Brittany, where she gave birth to a son they named Astrolabe. (They placed the boy in the care of Abelard's sister Denise.) Abelard proposed marriage, and Fulbert was agreeable—not least because he would have one of the most admired men in France for an adoptive son-in-law. Surprisingly, it was Héloïse who objected, on the grounds that marriage would ruin Abelard's chances for advancement in the church, and that family responsibilities would keep him from his work. Furthermore, she maintained that their love was stronger than any legal vows.

Nevertheless, they went ahead with the marriage, which they kept secret to protect Abelard's reputation. Soon, however, Fulbert began bragging about the fact that Abelard was his relative, and when the two publicly denied that they were married, Fulbert became abusive toward his niece. Abelard arranged for Héloïse to escape to a convent, or nunnery, in Argenteuil (ar-zhahn-TWEE).

Fearing that Abelard intended to force Héloïse to become a nun, thereby breaking off the marriage, Fulbert decided to take revenge. He bribed Abelard's servant to leave his master's door unlocked, and one night Fulbert, accompanied by a few hoodlums, broke into Abelard's bedroom and castrated him.

Despite the many enemies he had made, Abelard had many friends as well, and the public was outraged when they learned what had happened. Abelard's servant and one of Fulbert's henchmen were captured, blinded, and castrated; as for Fulbert, he lost his position and was forced to leave the city.

New enemies

Feeling that his misfortune was a punishment from God, Abelard became a monk in 1119, and told Héloïse to become a nun. But soon he was back to his rebellious self, raising hackles among the monks at the monastery of Saint-Denis by criticizing their methods. Therefore when he requested permission to return to his work as a teacher, the monks were happy to see him go.

In 1120, Abelard wrote a book about the nature of the Trinity that so infuriated some of Anselm's disciples that they organized a meeting at Soissons (swah-SAWn) in 1121 and condemned him on religious grounds. Abelard returned to the monastery, but again made enemies, and with the help of a powerful friend established a monastery of his own dedicated to the Paraclete, or Holy Ghost. This caused problems too, since monasteries were supposed to be dedicated to the entire Trinity or to Christ.

In 1123, Abelard published one of his most important works, *Sic et Non* ("For and Against"), which presented some 160 seemingly illogical statements by church leaders and argued that only through reasoning could one understand them. It was bad enough to place such an emphasis on reason as opposed to religious faith, but also in 1123, his *Ethics* put forth the idea that sin is a matter of one's intentions rather than one's actions; in other words, a sin can only be a sin if one knowingly commits it. Students continued to flock to Abelard, but when he realized he had gained a truly powerful enemy in **Bernard of Clairvaux** (see entry), he took a job in Brittany—far from Paris.

Abelard's latter years

In 1128, Héloïse established a convent in the buildings formerly occupied by Abelard's monastery. Meanwhile Abelard's enemies in Brittany tried several times to have him killed, so he escaped and in 1132 wrote a volume translated as *The Story of My Misfortunes*. Héloïse obtained a copy and wrote him a letter in which she made it clear that she still loved him. Abelard responded: "If ... you have need of my instruction and writings in matters pertaining to God, write to me what you want, so that I may answer as God permits me." She understood that he no longer wanted to speak of love, but they continued to correspond on questions of faith.

By 1136, Abelard was back in Paris, preparing to debate Bernard. But Bernard was not about to engage in an argument he knew he would lose, and on June 3, 1140, he charged Abelard with heresy (HAIR-uh-see)—that is, holding ideas that went against established church beliefs. Abelard appealed to Pope Innocent II (ruled 1130–43), but he learned that the pope supported Bernard, so he agreed to make peace. In private, however, he wrote a work the English title of which is *Dialogue of a Philosopher with a Jew and a Christian*. In it he still maintained that reason, as opposed to blind faith, was a necessary part of religious belief.

By this time, Abelard was sixty-three and in ailing health. He died on April 21, 1142, and in accordance with his wishes, was buried at the Paraclete. When Héloïse died twenty-two years later, she was laid to rest beside him. Later their bodies were moved to Père-Lachaise (PAYR luh-SHEZ), a famous cemetery in Paris, where their headstone reads, "ABELARD: HÉLOÏSE—For Ever One."

For More Information

Books

Encyclopedia of World Biography, second edition. Detroit: Gale, 1998.

Skuryznski, Gloria. *Spider's Voice* (fiction). New York: Atheneum Books for Young Readers, 1999.

Web Sites

"Abelard and Heloise Links." [Online] Available http://maple.lemoyne. edu/~kagan/abld.htm (last accessed July 26, 2000).

"Li Po." [Online] Available http://www.dpo.uab.edu/~yangzw/libai1. html (last accessed July 26, 2000).

"Peter Abelard." [Online] Available http://www.mala.bc.ca/~mcneil/ abelard.htm (last accessed July 26, 2000).

"Peter Abelard, Abbot, Theologian, Philosopher." [Online] Available http://justus.anglican.org/resources/bio/142.html (last accessed July 26, 2000).

Ala-ud-din Muhammad Khalji

Born 1200s
Died 1316

Indian sultan

Ala-ud-din was one of the most noteworthy of India's Muslim rulers during the Middle Ages. Although Hinduism and not Islam (the religion of Muslims) is the majority religion in India, Muslim invasions in the 700s and afterwards spread the faith throughout the subcontinent, so that by Ala-ud-din's time Islam dominated the land politically if not in terms of population. Ala-ud-din launched an ambitious and bloody campaign of conquest that took him deep into southern India—and might have gone on to even more far-flung campaigns if he had not wisely heeded the suggestions of his advisors.

Muslims and Hindus

Today the Indian subcontinent is divided into several countries, most notably India, Pakistan, and Bangladesh. The latter two, in the west and east, respectively, have Muslim majorities, whereas India's population is overwhelmingly Hindu. It would be hard to imagine two religions more different than Islam, which worships a single God, and Hinduism,

"The usual policy of the Sultans was clearly sketched by Ala-ud-din, who required his advisers to draw up 'rules and regulations for grinding down the Hindus, and for depriving them of that wealth and property which fosters disaffection and rebellion.'"

Will Durant, Our Oriental Heritage

Hindu and Buddhist Rulers of India

Throughout the Middle Ages, there were numerous Hindu- and Buddhist-dominated kingdoms in India, primarily in the central and southern portions of the subcontinent. These have received far less attention than their Muslim counterparts, largely because the southern realms were not significantly connected to events outside the country. By contrast, the Delhi Sultanate was religiously linked with the Middle East and confronted invasions by the Mongols and Tamerlane.

Nonetheless, it is fascinating to study Hindu dominions such as the Chalukya (KUH-luh-kyuh) empire, which rose and fell periodically between about 600 and about 1200. Most notable among the rulers of the Chalukya, who controlled the Deccan Plateau of central India, was Pulakesin II (pul-uh-KAY-shin; ruled 610–42). Like his foe Harsha (see box in Mansa Musa entry), against whom he scored a victory in 620, Pulakesin received a visit from the Chinese pilgrim Hsüan-tsang.

Among the kingdoms with which Pulakesin did battle was that of the Pallava dynasty. The latter ruled southern India from about 300 to about 900, and established settlements in the Malay lands of Southeast Asia. The Pallavas were overtaken by the Cholas, a dynasty of Tamils from Ceylon who controlled southern India from about 900 to about 1200.

Most notable among the Chola rulers were a father and son, Rajaraja I (ruled 985–1014) and Rajendra (ruled 1014–44). Rajaraja built their empire into a large and unified one, defeating a number of other kingdoms along the way. He was also the first significant ruler of India to employ naval forces, which he used for conquests of Ceylon and the Maldive Islands. Rajendra extended Chola rule far into the north of India, up to the Ganges River, and conducted extensive trade with Southeast Asia.

with its many gods. In large part because of the clash between Hinduism and Islam, India was separated into Hindu and Muslim nations when it achieved independence in 1947.

The roots of Hinduism in India go back thousands of years, but Islam only entered the country with an invasion by forces from the Middle East in 711. Thus began the first of many Muslim dynasties in India, this one a short-lived sultanate in what is now Pakistan. These Muslim invasions took place primarily in the north; in southern India, Hindu and Buddhist kingdoms prevailed (see box).

The Delhi Sultanate

During the late 900s, successive waves of Turkish invaders established their power in the cities of Lahore (now in Pakistan) and Delhi. One of the Turks' slaves was Qutb-ud-Din Aybak (küt-büd-DEEN eye-BAHK) who achieved his independence and in 1206 became ruler over an empire centered at Delhi. This marked the founding of the Delhi Sultanate, the first independent Muslim kingdom in India, with no ties to an outside ruler.

In 1290, the Khalji (kal-JEE) family began thirty years of control over the sultanate. The most important Khalji ruler, and the one who held the throne for the majority of those three decades, was the ruthless Ala-ud-din Muhammad (uh-LAH-ood-deen).

Taking control of the sultanate

Little is known about Ala-ud-din's life until the sultan—his uncle and father-in-law—appointed him governor of

Muslims pray at Jama Masjid, India's largest mosque, during the holy month of Ramadan in January 2000. Islam is not the majority religion in India today, but in Ala-ud-din's time, it was politically dominant. *Reproduced by permission of the Corbis Corporation.*

Kara, a state within the sultanate, in 1292. Three years later, Ala-ud-din marched on a number of enemy cities, and began making plans to overthrow his father-in-law.

Ala-ud-din moved farther south than any Muslim conqueror yet had when, in 1296, his troops plunged into the Deccan Plateau that forms the center of India. There they defeated a Hindu raja, or lord, in the region of Devagiri (day-vah-GEER-ee). As a result of this victory Ala-ud-din seized 17,250 pounds of gold, 200 pounds of pearls, and 28,250 pounds of silver. His men, buoyed by their success, supported him in his march to the capital, where he had his father-in-law killed and declared himself the sultan.

Wars of conquest

The next fifteen years, from 1296 to 1311, were spent on a seemingly endless series of wars in which Ala-ud-din sought to gain control over southern India. He dealt severely with Hindu rajas whenever his forces clashed with theirs, and adopted the Muslim practice of treating a war of conquest as a *jihad* or "holy war."

By 1303, he had subdued most of the powerful kingdoms in north central India. Then he turned his attention to fighting back the Mongols, who were trying to invade the country from the northwest, and this took three years of his time. He then turned his attention to conquering central India, and by 1309 his forces had reached the southernmost tip of the subcontinent.

Alexander II

It had been centuries since any ruler had achieved this feat. Ala-ud-din was compared to Alexander the Great (356–323 B.C.), the Greek conqueror who subdued more land in a shorter period of time than any general before or since. Alexander had special significance to India, since it was there that his wars of conquest had stopped. Alexander's example, in fact, had spawned the creation of India's first large empire under the Mauryans (324–184 B.C.), who united much of the country.

Conscious of Alexander's example, and of his reputation, Ala-ud-din issued coins that referred to him as "Alexander II." From his position of glory as ruler over most of the subcontinent, he considered an ambitious plan of world conquest. His advisors, however, told him that his energies would be better spent on consolidating his rule than on trying to conquer new lands.

Ala-ud-din wisely listened to his counselors. Certainly he had plenty of reason not to risk his gains, since he was already the wealthiest sultan in the history of Delhi. He did toy with the idea of starting a new religion—presumably one based on himself—but turned from this vain scheme to the serious business of running an empire.

Ala-ud-din's authoritarian state

The rule of Ala-ud-din was tyrannical and authoritarian, making use of secret police and spies. Known for his harsh treatment of enemies, he was particularly cruel toward Hindus, who he considered enemies of Allah. He imposed severe taxes on them, and forbade them to possess weapons or ride horses.

Muhammad ibn Tughluq

The dynasty that replaced the Khaljis four years after Ala-ud-din's death was the Tughluq (tug-LUK) family. Its most notorious member was Muhammad ibn Tughluq (c. 1290–1351), who assumed the throne in 1325.

Like Ala-ud-din, Tughluq was known for his ruthless treatment of Hindus, and the harsh measures he used to suppress rebellions. He once punished a rebellious noble by having the man skinned alive and cooked with rice; he then sent the remains to the man's wife and children—and the noble happened to be his cousin.

Yet Tughluq, who hosted the visiting traveler Ibn Battuta (see box in Marco Polo entry), proved a less effective ruler than Ala-ud-din. He lost both territory and influence during his reign, weakening the Delhi Sultanate and hastening its eventual downfall at the hands of **Tamerlane** (see entry) in 1398. Tughluq himself lost his life during an expedition against rebels in 1351.

On the other hand, Ala-ud-din cultivated the arts, making Delhi a city more splendid than ever before. Thanks to the Mongols' invasions of the Middle East and Central Asia, waves of wealthy and talented Muslim refugees had poured into Delhi; and this, combined with the wealth he had gathered in his wars of conquest, helped Ala-ud-din turn the city into a center of learning and culture.

Ala-ud-din also built a number of lasting monuments, even as his own life was fading away. Years of hard living had caught up with him, and in his last years he was weak both physically and mentally, allowing himself to be dominated by one of his generals. He died in January 1316, and the Khalji dynasty ended just four years later.

For More Information

Books

Brace, Steve. *India*. Des Plaines, IL: Heinemann Library, 1999.

Dolicini, Donatella and Francesco Montessoro. *India in the Islamic Era and Southeast Asia (8th to 19th Century)*. Illustrated by Giorgio Bacchin and Gianni de Conmo, translated by Pamela Swinglehurst. Austin, TX: Raintree Steck-Vaughn, 1997.

Durant, Will. *The Story of Civilization,* Volume I: *Our Oriental Heritage*. New York: Simon and Schuster, 1954.

Ganeri, Anita. *Exploration into India*. New York: Discovery, 1994.

Schulberg, Lucille. *Historic India*. New York: Time-Life Books, 1968.

Web Sites

"Delhi—India: History & Times." [Online] Available http://www.delhiindia.com/history.html (last accessed July 26, 2000).

"History of India—Ancient: The Chola Empire." *History of India*. [Online] Available http://www.historyofindia.com/chola.html (last accessed July 26, 2000).

"Itihaas: Medieval: End of Delhi Sultanate." *Itihaas*. [Online] Available http://www.itihaas.com/medieval/delhi-sultanate.html (last accessed July 26, 2000).

Alexander Nevsky

Born 1220
Died 1263

Russian prince and hero

Numbered among the greatest of Russia's heroes, Alexander Nevsky saved his country many times, both in battle with invaders from the west, and later by negotiating with the Mongols. The defeat of the Teutonic Knights of Germany was a particularly dramatic event, a battle on ice that would form a memorable scene in a 1938 film about Alexander's defense of Russia. By contrast, the role Alexander took with regard to the Mongols seemed like a case of giving in to a foreign invader. Yet he had little choice, and in retrospect it seems certain that he acted wisely.

The many Russias

Russia first emerged as a political entity in about 900 under the leadership of Kiev (kee-YEV), a city-state that is now the capital of Ukraine. Thus historians refer to the country during this period as "Kievan Russia," though in fact Russia was far from a single, unified nation. It was instead a collection of city-states—actually duchies, or regions controlled by dukes—that were sometimes at war with one another and sometimes at peace.

"Let the manly images of our great ancestors [such as] Alexander Nevsky ... inspire you in this war!"

From a speech by Soviet dictator Josef Stalin following the German invasion of Russia in 1941

Portrait: *Reproduced by permission of Hulton-Getty/Tony Stone Images.*

Most of these political units were strictly controlled by princes, but the northern city-states of Novgorod (NAWV-guh-rud) and Pskov (SKAWV) had more relaxed governments, at least by Russian standards. There, in a region close to other lands in Northern Europe, business interests had an influential role in easing the traditionally harsh control of Russian leaders.

After 1054, Kievan Russia began to disintegrate, and more than a century of turmoil followed. By the late 1100s, however, at least a measure of stability returned as the Grand Duchy of Vladimir-Suzdal (VLAH-duh-meer SÜZ-duhl) assumed leadership.

Surrounded by enemies

To the east of Vladimir were the Volga Bulgars, a group of Turks who had settled in the region, and with whom the Russians maintained an uneasy peace. To the northwest were the Germans, Danes, and Swedes on the Baltic Sea, along with Letts or Latvians and Estonians; and to the west was Lithuania, then a significant power. At a time when religion dictated political allegiance, the Russians, who had embraced the Greek Orthodox Church, found themselves faced with enemies on many sides: the Muslims in the east, and the Catholics in the west and northwest.

Early in the 1200s came a new wave of potential enemies, a group who embraced no religion the Russians even recognized: the Mongols, whose leader was **Genghis Khan** (see entry). When the Mongols attacked the Volga Bulgars, the Russians were divided as to which side they should take, with some states coming to the aid of their neighbors. The princes of Vladimir stayed out of the fight.

Mongol invasion

Then, in 1237, Genghis Khan's nephew Batu Khan swept over the Bulgars and conquered several Russian cities—including Vladimir. The Russian prince Yuri led the defense of Russia, but was killed in the fight, and the Mongols kept moving toward Novgorod, one of the most valued of the Russian states.

Then, as suddenly as they had appeared, the Mongols turned away. The cause was probably the spring thaw, which turned the hard ground into mud that made it hard to cross. The Mongols made a vast camp on the Volga River, which would serve as their base for many years to come. By 1240, they were on the move again, razing Kiev and marching deep into Europe, where they overcame Polish and German forces to conquer Hungary.

They had nearly reached Vienna, Austria, in 1241 when suddenly they turned back again. This time the reason was that the ruling khan, or chieftain (Genghis's successor) had died, and Batu rushed back to Mongolia to ensure that he got a piece of the inheritance. Thus Europe was saved from Mongol conquest, but the Mongols put down roots in Russia, where their empire became known as the "Golden Horde." "Horde" is the English version of the Mongols' word for their huge encampments, *orda;* and "golden" signified the great wealth the Mongols had gained through conquest.

Mongol rule in Russia was an established fact. Thus in 1238, when Yuri's brother Yaroslav II (yuh-ruh-SLAHF) assumed leadership of the Russians, he had to gain the Mongols' approval before he could declare himself leader. The Mongols did not want the trouble of controlling Russia politically: they simply wanted to collect tribute, or taxes, and they needed Russian princes to ensure that the collection of these taxes—which included not only money but a tenth of each year's harvest—went smoothly.

Alexander becomes Nevsky

Taking advantage of the Mongols' weakening of Russia, the Swedes had invaded Russian lands in 1236 on the pretext that they were there to convert people from Eastern Orthodoxy to Catholicism. It was then that Alexander, son of Yaroslav, made his first mark on history. Born in Vladimir, he had been raised among the tumultuous events of the Mongol invasion, and was prepared for war. Thus at the age of sixteen, he led a force that met the Swedes in battle on the River Neva (NAY-vah) on July 15, 1236. It was a small victory, but it made Alexander's name: from then on he would be known as Alexander of the Neva, or Alexander Nevsky.

Heroes of Catholic Europe

Americans sometimes mistakenly lump all of Eastern Europe together, primarily because after World War II (1939–45), most of its nations fell under communist dictatorships allied with the Soviet Union. In fact, there is a sharp distinction between Eastern European nations that accepted Greek Orthodoxy during the Middle Ages, and those that became Roman Catholic. Orthodox lands, such as Russia, Bulgaria, and Serbia, adopted the alphabet of **St. Cyril** (see dual entry with St. Methodius), and tended to have more rigid governments. Catholic lands, among them Hungary, Poland, and the modern Czech Republic, were more closely tied with Western traditions.

One of the first important leaders of Catholic Eastern Europe was St. Wenceslas (WIN-suh-slaws; c. 907–929), prince of Bohemia—roughly equivalent to the Czech Republic. His grandmother raised him as a Christian, but his mother maintained old pagan traditions, and later had the grandmother killed. Wenceslas remained faithful to Catholicism, however, and encouraged the sending of missionaries to convert the Germans, many of whom still maintained pagan religions. Known for his kindness and his devotion to God, Wenceslas (the subject of the Christmas song "Good King Wenceslas") was killed by his brother Boreslav, who wanted to take the throne. Soon after his death, he was declared a martyr, or someone who has died for the faith, and was made a saint. It is interesting to note that the name Wenceslas in the Czech language is Václav (VAHK-luv), and that after the Czech Republic threw off communism in the 1990s, its first president was the poet Václav Havel (HAHV-ul).

Having proven himself, the teenaged Alexander was given control over Novgorod, which was soon threatened by German invaders. These were the Teutonic (too-TAHN-ik) or German Knights, a group that had been formed as a semi-religious order, but whose real business was war and conquest. In the winter of 1242, Alexander and his brother Andrew raised a force from Novgorod to meet the invaders.

The "Battle on the Ice"

Winters in northern Russia are long, and the surface of Lake Chudskoe was still frozen when the Russian force marched out to meet the Germans, along with their Finnish

King Stephen I of Hungary (977–1038) also grew up in a world heavily influenced by paganism, but accepted Catholicism in 997. This meant that his people also accepted Catholicism, a fact that excited Pope Sylvester II. In his haste to crown a new Christian king in 1000, Sylvester sent Stephen a crown bearing a cross that was slightly bent. This remained the crown of Hungary—even appearing on the flag of the later Austro-Hungarian Empire—until 1918. In 1083, Stephen was declared a saint.

Another important Hungarian ruler was László I (LAHZ-loh; c. 1040–1095). In 1091, László conquered Croatia and Bosnia, and extended his rule into Transylvania. Facing a resurgence of paganism, he took measures to ensure that Catholicism regained strength in the country, and supported Pope **Gregory VII** in his conflicts with Holy Roman Emperor **Henry IV** (see dual entry). He also instituted a new legal code that helped restore order in Hungary, which had been troubled by years of internal conflict, and was later declared a saint.

Among the greatest of Poland's rulers was Casimir III (KAZ-uh-meer; 1310–1370), also known as Casimir the Great. Under his reign, Poland's territory and influence increased greatly, and he dealt successfully with both Bohemia and the same Teutonic Knights that had threatened Alexander Nevsky's Russia. Polish armies under Casimir even occupied Russia in the 1340s. Casimir instituted a series of laws, founded the University of Cracow, and ushered in a golden age of Polish history that lasted for some three hundred years.

allies, on April 5, 1242. In a scene made famous for modern filmgoers by the director Sergei Eisenstein, the invaders rushed at the defending Russians, who suddenly surprised them by closing ranks around the enemy and attacking them from the rear. The Russians scored a huge victory in the "Battle on the Ice," which became a legendary event in Russian history.

Two years later, Alexander drove off a Lithuanian invading force, and though he soon left Novgorod, the people there had become so dependent on his defense that they asked him to come back as their prince. With Novgorod now in the lead among Russian states, Alexander was the effective ruler of Russia.

Coexisting with the Mongols

As leader, Alexander faced a less dramatic, but much more important, challenge than he had when doing battle with the invaders of Novgorod: the question of whether, or how, to coexist with the Mongols. He could have chosen to resist, as other Russian princes did—and could have lost everything trying, as was the case with most of the others. Faced with this reality, as well as the fact that the Mongols were willing to leave the Greek Orthodox religion alone, whereas the Germans and others wanted to convert the Russians, Alexander chose coexistence.

Proclaimed Grand Prince of Vladimir in 1252, Alexander continued to deal with invasions from the west, but most of his energy was spent on the Mongols. He assisted them in carrying out a census, or a count of the people, as part of their aim to raise taxes on the Russians. He even executed other Russian leaders who resisted the Mongols' efforts at census-taking.

The foundations of modern Russia

Alexander died in 1263 and was succeeded by Andrew, who died a year later. Alexander's son Yaroslav then took control until 1272, and when he died he left the town of Moscow to his son Daniel. The latter, only two years old at the time, would grow up to build Moscow as a mighty force, and in time it would become the leading city of Russia.

Despite his cooperation with the Mongols, Alexander is remembered as a hero. In the 1700s, when the Mongols were long gone and Russia was emerging as a great power, Peter the Great, czar (ZAR) or emperor of Russia, built the city of St. Petersburg on the Neva. There he dedicated a shrine to Alexander, who had been named a saint in the Orthodox Church. In 1836, on the 600th anniversary of the Battle of the Neva, the principal street of St. Petersburg was named Nevsky Prospect in his honor.

Over one hundred years later, by which time Russia had become the Soviet Union under the dictatorship of Josef Stalin, the country faced the threat of another German invasion—this time by the Nazis under Adolf Hitler. It was then that Eisenstein made his famous film, with a memorable musical score by the great composer Sergei Prokofiev. The scene of the "Battle on the Ice" was a compelling one, and it sent a warning that Hitler chose not to heed.

For More Information

Books

Ayer, Eleanor H. *Poland: A Troubled Past, a New Start*. Tarrytown, NY: Benchmark Books, 1996.

Burke, Patrick. *Eastern Europe*. Austin, TX: Raintree Steck-Vaughn, 1997.

Hintz, Martin. *Poland*. New York: Children's Press, 1998.

Riordan, James. *Eastern Europe: The Lands and Their Peoples*. Morristown, NJ: Silver Burdett Press, 1987.

Sioras, Efstathia. *Czech Republic*. New York: Marshall Cavendish, 1999.

Steins, Richard. *Hungary: Crossroads of Europe*. New York: Benchmark Books, 1997.

Motion Pictures

Alexander Nevsky. BMG Video, 1938.

Web Sites

"Life of St. Alexander Nevsky." [Online] Available http://members. tripod.com/~shtyetz_john/life-of-st-alexander.html (last accessed July 26, 2000).

Temple of Alexander Nevsky. [Online] Available http://sangha.net/messen gers/nevsky.htm (last accessed July 26, 2000).

Augustine

Born 354
Died 430

North African church leader and philosopher

Aside from Jesus Christ and others from the New Testament, no one had as great an influence on the shaping of the Christian faith as Saint Augustine, who helped bridge the period between ancient and medieval times. He grew up in a world heavily influenced by the Roman Empire, but during his life the power of Rome became increasingly shaky, and he promoted Christian faith as a more stable foundation than any earthly kingdom.

Augustine served as bishop or church leader over the North African city of Hippo, and he wrote literally hundreds of books discussing specific aspects of Christianity. Many of the questions addressed by Augustine have long since been decided, but two of his works, *Confessions* and the *City of God*, remain classics with an eternal appeal.

Christians and pagans

He was born Aurelius Augustinus (aw-gu-STY-nus) on November 13, 354, but it was by the name Augustine (aw-

"Suddenly every vain hope became worthless to me, and with an incredible warmth of heart I ... began now to arise that I might return to thee.... How ardent was I then, my God, how ardent to fly from earthly things to thee!"

From the Confessions

Portrait: *Reproduced by permission of the Corbis Corporation.*

23

GUS-tin) that he would become famous. His hometown was Tagaste (tuh-GAS-tee), a city in what is now Algeria, which at that time was part of the Western Roman Empire.

Like many Romans, Augustine's father Patricius believed in the old Roman religion, which was pagan, meaning that its followers worshiped a variety of gods. Many other Romans, including Augustine's mother Monica, had accepted Christianity. The latter religion had developed in the three centuries following the deaths of Jesus and his followers, and had gained wide acceptance among the emperors of Rome.

As for young Augustine, he did not believe in the pagan gods, but he refused to accept Christianity either. He later recalled in the *Confessions,* a book detailing his experiences as a youth and his eventual acceptance of the Christian faith, that Monica prayed for him often during his wayward youth.

A reckless young man

Because Augustine's parents wanted their son to get ahead in life, they enrolled him at one of the best Roman schools, in the city of Madura. In 370, when he was sixteen years old, he completed his studies there, and hoped to go on to the equivalent of college. However, his father had to raise the money for his studies, so in the meantime, Augustine returned home. He spent a year in Tagaste, during which time he associated with other young men who encouraged him to engage in reckless living, including sexual activity, theft, and acts of destructiveness.

In 371, Augustine went away to Carthage to continue his studies. Located in what is now Tunisia, Carthage was the greatest city of Roman Africa—but it was also a place where a young person could get into a great deal of trouble. While there, Augustine became involved in a number of sexual relationships, one of which resulted in the birth of a son, Adeodatus (ay-dee-AHD-uh-tus). He also spent time with a gang of troublemakers called the "wreckers," and flirted with a faith called Manichaeism (man-uh-KEE-izm).

A religion which had originated in Persia or Iran, Manichaeism had many Christian elements. Yet it differed

sharply from Christianity in a number of other ways, most notably in Manichaeans' claim that they alone had special knowledge concerning the true nature of good and evil. Augustine would remain associated with the Manichaeans for nine years, and encouraged many of his friends to accept that faith. Despite his later rejection of Manichaeism, Augustine recognized that his interest in the religion was an early step in the quest for understanding that would lead him to Christianity.

A view of modern Carthage, Tunisia. In Augustine's time, Carthage was the greatest city of Roman Africa and Augustine's home for many years. *Photograph by Jason Laure. Reproduced by permission of Laure Communications.*

On to Rome

Patricius, who became a Christian on his deathbed, died in 372; however, a wealthy man named Romanianus agreed to support Augustine in the completion of his education. When he finished his schooling in 374, at age twenty, Augustine returned to Tagaste, where he planned to teach. However, when Monica learned that her son was a Manichee, she refused to allow him into her home, so he returned to Carthage.

Augustine remained in Carthage for a few years, but he knew that if he really wanted to make a good career for himself, he would have to get closer to Rome itself. Therefore in the fall of 383, he moved to the northern Italian city of Milan (mi-LAHN), where he got an important job as a teacher of rhetoric, the art of speaking and writing. Though he was well on his way to great success, he found that something was lacking in his life, and he became deeply depressed. In the midst of his unhappiness, he reached out for the faith of his mother: Christianity.

From convert to bishop

In fact Monica herself had by then come to Italy, and she was a great influence on Augustine during this time of searching. So was Ambrose (339–397), the bishop of Milan, another key figure in the establishment of medieval Christianity. But perhaps the greatest influence on Augustine's conversion was his direct reading of the Bible itself, which he undertook after hearing a child at play chanting "Pick up and read, pick up and read." In July 386, Augustine converted to Christianity, and on Easter Sunday 387 was baptized, or lowered into water as a symbol of death and rebirth in Christ.

Soon after his conversion, Augustine planned to go back to Africa, but he had to go alone: just before the time they were supposed to leave, Monica became sick and died—but she died happy, knowing that her son had become a Christian. In 388, he established a monastery, a place for men who wanted to escape the outside world and spend a quiet life searching for spiritual understanding, in Tagaste. Augustine, however, was not destined to have a quiet life. In 391, while visiting the nearby town of Hippo, he became a priest, and five years later became the bishop of Hippo.

Addressing religious disputes

During the years that followed, Augustine would face a number of disputes between mainstream Christianity

Simeon Stylites the Elder

Like Augustine, Simeon Stylites the Elder (SIM-ee-un stuh-LIT-eez; c. 388–459) was later named a saint—that is, someone officially recognized by the church for their holiness. Yet whereas Augustine lived a life closely tied to the central events of his time, Simeon was an offbeat figure at the fringes of society. The name *Stylites* is a variation on a Greek word meaning "pillar-hermit," and in fact Simeon was the most famous of these men, who went out into the desert and lived atop tall pillars or columns.

Simeon was born in northern Syria in about 388, and he spent his childhood and teen years working as a shepherd boy. At age sixteen, he decided to become a monk—someone who leaves the outside world to search for spiritual understanding in a center called a monastery. Many monks engage in self-denial, for instance by going without food for long periods of time, but Simeon took things much further. He wrapped a rope tightly around his body and lived that way for more than a year, until his flesh rotted and no one could stand to be near him because of the smell. When the abbot, leader of the monastery, inspected Simeon's bed and found it covered with maggots, he ordered him to leave the monastery.

Simeon spent three years living in a hut, where he pushed himself to ever more difficult feats, for instance by standing for long periods. When this proved too easy, he forced himself to live atop a cliff in the desert. By then, however, word of Simeon's impressive self-denial—which many interpreted as a sign of great devotion to God—had spread throughout the area, and followers came seeking spiritual wisdom. Determined to remove himself from the world, Simeon arranged for the erection of a pillar with a small platform on top. It was there he would live for the remainder of his life.

Initially, Simeon's pillar was about nine feet high, but over time it was replaced by increasingly taller ones; by the time of his death he was living on a column fifty or sixty feet high. Followers still came to him, climbing a ladder along the side, and his many admirers included Roman emperors and bishops. After thirty years atop the pillar, Simeon died on September 2, 459.

and other versions of the faith. Among his first opponents were the Manichaeans, and in this conflict Augustine found himself pitted against old friends. Some, such as Honoratus (for whom he wrote a book called *On the Virtue of Believing* in order to explain Christian faith), converted to Christianity; others, including Fortunatus—subject of a book by Augustine called *Against Fortunatus the Manichee*—did not.

After Augustine won a public debate with the Manichaean leader Felix in 404, Manichaeism ceased to be a significant force in Hippo.

Another threat came from the Donatists (DOH-nuh-tistz), a North African splinter group who rejected the mainstream church leadership—that is, the bishop of Rome, who became known as the pope. Beginning in 410, Augustine also squared off with the Pelagians (puh-LAY-jee-unz). Their leader, Pelagius (c. 354–c. 418), taught that humanity was born without sin, and did not need the help of God to achieve goodness. This directly contradicted mainstream Christianity, which held that all humans were sinful in the absence of God. Augustine led the fight against Pelagianism with works such as *On the Merits of Sinners and Forgiveness* (411).

In his latter days, Augustine found himself in conflict not only with the Pelagians, but with groups around the Christian world who embraced the idea of predestination (pree-des-ti-NAY-shun). Predestination is the belief that a person's ultimate fate—that is, whether they will go to Heaven or Hell—is already decided before their birth. It has some basis in the Bible, but so too does the idea of free will, or the belief that humans have complete freedom to choose whether or not they will follow God. Augustine set out to demonstrate that free will and predestination were both true, and furthermore that predestination did not give people a license to sin.

City of God

In his early years as the bishop of Hippo, Augustine had written the *Confessions*. This work could properly be called the first real autobiography, or personal history, because it is not nearly as concerned with outside events as it is with the inner life of Augustine himself. It is one of Augustine's two greatest contributions to literature, the second being *City of God*, which he wrote between 413 and 425.

The event that inspired the writing of the latter book was the sacking, or destruction, of Rome by an invading tribe called the Visigoths in 410. In hindsight, historians recognize the sacking of Rome as the beginning of the end of the Western Roman Empire, which ceased to exist in 476; at the time, people viewed it as the worst disaster in the history of the world. Believers in Rome's pagan religion blamed Christians, saying that the destruction of the city was a punishment from the gods.

Augustine took exactly the opposite position: the destruction of Rome, he said, was God's punishment for the Romans' persisting belief in their old pagan religion. In *City of God,* he pointed out many examples in Roman history when the people had called on the gods' help, but to no avail. Perhaps drawing on his past belief in Manichaeism, which viewed the world as an eternal struggle between good and evil, Augustine now explained all of existence as a conflict between the "City of God," or the church, and the "City of Man"—that is, the belief systems that opposed Christianity.

Facing the end of the ancient world

As Augustine was writing *On the Predestination of the Saints* in 429, shadows were gathering over the world he knew. A tribe called the Vandals, who like the Visigoths were barbarians or uncivilized people, had conquered Spain, and in the spring of 429 the Vandals launched an attack on Africa. By the wintertime, they had begun a siege, or sustained military attack, against Hippo. On August 28, 430, while the Vandals were besieging the city, Augustine died.

The Vandals would later launch such a vicious attack on Rome itself that their name became a synonym for reckless destructiveness. Yet even they respected the name of Augustine: when they captured and destroyed the city in 431, they allowed a library containing his books to remain standing.

The fact that Christian beliefs are so clearly established today is a tribute to the work of Augustine and others who lived in a time when basic issues had not yet been decided. In his own life, he saw the rapid decline of Roman civilization and the beginnings of the barbarian triumph that would plunge Western Europe into centuries of confusion. His work helped Christians weather this painful transition.

For More Information

Books

De Zeeuw, P. *Augustine, the Farmer's Boy of Tagaste.* Pella, IA: Inheritance Publications, 1998.

Farjeon, Eleanor. *Ten Saints.* Illustrations by Helen Sewell. New York: H. Z. Walck, 1958.

Hansel, Robert R. *The Life of Saint Augustine.* New York: F. Watts, 1968.

Web Sites

"St. Augustine." *Island of Freedom.* [Online] Available http://www.island-of-freedom.com/AUGUST.HTM (last accessed July 26, 2000).

"St. Augustine of Hippo." [Online] Available http://www.geocities.com/Athens/1534/august.html (last accessed July 26, 2000).

Averroës

Born 1126
Died 1198

Spanish-Arab philosopher

As a thinker, Averroës represented the pinnacle of Islamic civilization in Spain; he was also the last of his line. Though devoutly committed to the beliefs of Islam, he placed great value on the workings of human reason, and in his many writings sought to explain how it was possible to be a person of both faith and thought. Unbeknownst to him, he would exert his greatest influence in the Christian lands of Western Europe, where his legacy brought about a renewed interest in the writings of the ancient Greek philosopher Aristotle.

The world of Averroës's birth

His name at birth was Abu al-Walid Muhammad ibn Ahmad ibn Muhammad ibn Rushd, and to this day he is known in the Arab world as ibn Rushd (IB'n RÜSH't). In the West, however, he is best known by the "Latinized" version of his name, Averroës (uh-VEER-uh-weez).

Averroës was born in the Spanish city of Córdoba in 1126, at a time when Spain had long been ruled by Muslims.

"Motion is eternal and continuous; all motion has its cause in a preceding motion. Without motion there is no time. We cannot conceive of motion having either a beginning or an end."

Commentary on Aristotle's Physics

The first caliphs, or rulers, had come from the Arabian dynasty of Umayyads (oo-MY-edz), but in 1086 they had been replaced by the Almoravids (al-mohr-AHV-idz) from Morocco. In 1120, just before Averroës's birth, another group of Moors called the Almohads had overthrown the Almoravids.

The double life of the Almohads

Each successive wave of invaders had been less cultured, and more inclined to demand that their people maintain an unwavering belief in the principles of Islam handed down by the prophet **Muhammad** (see entry). Each had in turn been softened by the refined, sophisticated ways of the brilliant Spanish Muslim civilization. This softening had contributed to the overthrow of the Umayyads, and then of the Almoravids; therefore the Almohads, determined to hold on to power, had to lead double lives.

Inside the houses of the caliphs and other powerful figures, men were privately permitted to use their minds, and to discuss the great questions of philosophy, or the study of the underlying meaning of the world. Among the lower classes, however, no deviation from hard-line Islam was permitted. In this way, the rulers hoped to preserve their power over the people. It was the destiny of Averroës, on the one hand a philosopher, and on the other hand an Islamic judge or *qadi* (KAH-dee), to live such a double life.

Both his grandfather and father had been qadis, and when Averroës came of age, he accepted the family calling. He not only studied law, but also medicine and a variety of other subjects, and it was probably during his early years that he first became intrigued by philosophy.

An audience with the caliph

At the age of thirty, Averroës went to Marrakech in Morocco. The latter was the capital of the Almohad caliphate, a realm that included what is now Spain and Portugal, as well as all of North Africa to the west of Egypt and the north of the Sahara Desert. A few years after Averroës moved to Marrakech, 'Abd al-Mu'mim, the caliph who had subdued much of this empire, died and was replaced by his son, Abu Ya'qub Yusuf (ruled 1163–1184).

In about 1169, the scholar Ibn Tufayl (too-FYL; c. 1105–1184) introduced Averroës to the young caliph. It was said that on their first meeting, Abu Ya'qub Yusuf, knowing about Averroës's wisdom, tried to engage him in a discussion of the ancient Greek philosophers. Aware of the strict rules against "ungodly" forms of learning, Averroës kept his mouth shut, but was amazed when the caliph turned to Ibn Tufayl and began engaging in a learned discourse. As a result, Averroës felt safe to embark on a lively discussion with the caliph, who was so impressed with his learning that he called on Averroës to become his teacher.

Commentaries on Aristotle

Abu Ya'qub Yusuf commented that the existing translations of Aristotle were inadequate. As a result, Averroës undertook the translations himself, and this led to a series of books that would make his fame.

Considered by many to be the greatest of the Greek philosophers, Aristotle (384–322 B.C.) wrote on a wide range of subjects. In the realm of philosophy itself, for instance, he examined matters such as logic, or the system of correct reasoning, and metaphysics, or the fundamental nature of being. He was also concerned with psychology, literature, and drama, and as a scientist his achievements in areas ranging from physics to botany were many and varied. Aristotle's work represented a past high point in human thought, the "Golden Age" of Greece, when great minds explored the frontiers of possibility.

In contrast to Aristotle, Averroës was not an original thinker; rather, he was, as later admirers called him, "The Great Commentator," whose greatest contribution lay in helping others understand Aristotle's thought. This was particularly valuable because, in the confusion that had attended the fall of the Western Roman Empire—and with it the virtual collapse of European civilization—much of the learning from ancient times had been lost.

Averroës was handicapped by the fact that he read no Greek, and therefore had to rely on second- or third-hand translations into Arabic. Yet he managed to overcome much of the misunderstanding that had plagued earlier scholars of Aristotle. Many of these had confused Aristotle's ideas with those of his teacher, Plato, an equally brilliant figure whose views were almost exactly opposite of Aristotle's. Averroës, in his commentaries, helped to separate that which was truly Aristotle from things that later scholars had mistakenly attributed to him.

Other writings and ideas

Other than his many commentaries on Aristotle's works, such as the *Rhetoric, Poetics,* and *Nichomachean Ethics,* Averroës's writings included an encyclopedia of medical knowledge, which he wrote between 1162 and 1169. Further evidence of his interest in medicine was a commentary he wrote on Galen (c. A.D. 130–c. A.D. 200), a Greek physician in the Roman Empire who was the ancient world's last great scientist.

Averroës remained committed to the idea that man could apply his intellect to problems and solve them through reasoning power. This may not sound like a groundbreaking concept, but in the twelfth century it was. One of Averroës's most important works, written between 1174 and 1180, was *The Incoherence of the Incoherence,* a response to attacks on philosophy by the hard-line Muslim theorist al-Ghazali (gah-ZAH-lee) in his 1095 book *The Incoherence of the Philosophers.*

Later generations of admirers in Europe, perhaps wishing to separate Averroës from his Muslim roots, overestimated the degree to which he revolted against mainstream Islam. He genuinely believed that there was no contradiction between learning and faith in Allah, a point he demonstrated in *On the Harmony of Religion and Philosophy,* also written in the period from 1174 to 1180.

Disgrace under al-Mansur

In 1169, the same year he began his friendship with Abu Ya'qub Yusuf, Averroës was appointed qadi of Seville, another great city of Muslim Spain. Two years later, he returned to his hometown of Córdoba as qadi, but spent much of the decade that followed traveling around the Almohad caliphate, probably on business for the caliph.

Following the retirement of Ibn Tufayl, Averroës went to Marrakech in 1182 to become Abu Ya'qub Yusuf's personal physician. The caliph died two years later and was succeeded by his son, Abu Yusuf Ya'qub, known as al-Mansur, or "The Victorious." Al-Mansur took a generally favorable view of Averroës, but in 1195, when he needed the support of the *fuqaha* (a group of highly conservative Islamic scholars), Averroës suffered as a result.

The reason for this switch of allegiance was the fact that the caliphate was in grave danger of attack from Christian forces in the north who were undertaking the Reconquista (ray-kawn-KEES-tah) or reconquest of Spain for Christianity. Desperate wartime situations sometimes create witch-hunt atmospheres, and so it was in Córdoba, where Averroës's books were publicly burned and Averroës himself was subjected to great scorn for his unorthodox ideas. It was a sign of how al-Mansur truly felt about Averroës, however, that his actual punishment—a very short exile in the town of Lucena (loo-SAYN-uh)—was minor.

The great Greek philosopher Aristotle. Through his translations of and commentaries on Aristotle's works, Averroës brought a greater understanding of Aristotle's ideas. *Reproduced by permission of the Corbis Corporation.*

The sunset of Spanish Islam

Later in 1195, the caliph ended Averroës's sentence practically before it began, and sent orders for the philosopher to rejoin his court in Marrakech. This reversal of positions resulted from the fact that al-Mansur no longer needed the help of the *fuqaha:* on July 19, 1195, he had scored a victory against the Christians at Allarcos (ah-YAHdr-kohs), a town between Córdoba and Toledo. So Averroës went to Marrakech, where he lived less than three more years. He died in 1198, and al-Mansur followed him by just a few months.

Priscian

The career of Priscian, who flourished in c. A.D. 500, had many parallels to Averroës's life. Whereas Averroës lived in a European country dominated by an African power, Priscian grew up in a part of North Africa dominated by Vandal invaders from Europe. Both men represented the end of a civilization—Arabic and Roman, respectively—and both men preserved the learning of the distant past for future generations.

Priscian was a grammarian, or a specialist in grammar—specifically, Latin grammar. Grammar textbooks, as every student knows, require the use of sentences as examples; but instead of making up his own sentences, Priscian used great quotes from the esteemed poets of Greece and Rome. Thus thanks to Priscian, a whole range of materials by writers such as Homer in the earliest days of Greece to the late Roman scholars were preserved at a time when barbarians were destroying important texts.

Priscian wrote a long poem concerning the Roman weights and measures, which provides an encyclopedic array of knowledge to students of Roman life. In addition, he produced at least one example of a panegyric (pan-uh-JY-rik), a highly popular form in the later Roman Empire. Panegyrics were poems praising a ruler, in Priscian's case the Byzantine emperor Anastasius. Priscian's most significant work, however, was the sixteen-book *Institutiones grammaticae,* which became a classic grammar text used by **Alcuin** (see English Scholars, Thinkers, and Writers entry) and others in the Middle Ages.

Though it seemed that al-Mansur had saved the caliphate, in fact Allarcos was the last significant victory by Muslim armies in Spain. Fourteen years later, in 1212, the Spanish Christians scored a decisive victory at Las Navas de Tolosa, which effectively ended Moorish rule in Spain.

The brilliance of Muslim civilization had long before faded away in its homelands of Arabia, Syria, Iraq, and Persia far to the east. For a time, Islamic culture had thrived in the west, thanks to the successive caliphates that ruled Morocco and the Iberian Peninsula. Now that flame, too, had gone out; but in a turn of events that would have probably surprised Averroës, the torch of his ideas was passed to Christian Europe.

Ever since Christians reconquered Toledo in 1085, Western Europeans had taken a renewed interest in the ancient treasures of Greek, Hebrew, and Arabic learning preserved by the Spanish caliphate. This interest had grown over subsequent years, and when the Reconquista brought a new flood of works by Averroës and others into Christendom, these were met with enthusiasm. Soon translations of Averroës's work appeared in English, German, and Italian, and more were to follow. Averroës would have an enormous impact on Europe in the years to come—and there was an irony in that, because as a devout Muslim, he would have had little admiration for the societies that admired him.

For More Information

Books

Curtius, Ernst R. *European Literature and the Latin Middle Ages.* Translated by William R. Trask. New York: Harper and Row, 1963.

Hitti, Philip K. *Makers of Arab History.* New York: St. Martin's Press, 1968.

Peters, F. E. *Aristotle and the Arabs: The Aristotelian Tradition in Islam.* New York: New York University Press, 1969.

Web Sites

"Averroës As a Physician." [Online] Available http://www.levity.com/alchemy/islam21.html (last accessed July 26, 2000).

"Muslim Scientists and Islamic Civilization." [Online] Available http://users.erols.com/zenithco/index.html (last accessed July 26, 2000).

Basil II

Born 957
Died 1025

Byzantine emperor and conqueror

Ruler of the Byzantine Empire from 976 to 1025, a time when the power of the Muslim caliphate had faded and the Seljuk Turks had not yet made their impact, Basil II brought his realm to its greatest height since the time of **Justinian** (see entry). His story shares certain themes with that of England's King Alfred and Mali's Sundiata Keita (see boxes): in each case, the ruler of a beleaguered people led them in wars of conquest that united them and brought them to new glories. As leader of a world power, Basil would have the most impact of the three, but his victories would also be the most short-lived.

An unlikely hero

Unattractive and uneducated, Basil made an unlikely hero in Greek society, which placed a high emphasis on physical beauty and learning. Given the fact that he was raised in the imperial palace—he was the son of Emperor Romanus II (roh-MAIN-us; ruled 939–63)—his lack of education is hard to understand; so, too, is the fact that he never married.

"Basil II was the greatest military genius and the greatest military organizer of his time, one of the greatest of all time."

Romilly Jenkins, Byzantium: The Imperial Centuries A.D. 610–1071

Portrait: *Reproduced by permission of the Library of Congress.*

King Alfred the Great

Many rulers have been given the title "the Great," usually after their lifetime; Alfred (848–c. 900), however, was the only king of England ever assigned this distinguished title. In fact he was the first monarch to unite all of England under his rule: before Alfred's time, the land was divided among a number of smaller kingdoms, ruled either by Angles, Saxons, or Jutes. His own Saxon kingdom of Wessex was just one of these competing states.

The one unifying factor in these lands was religion, thanks in large part to the missionaries sent by Pope **Gregory I** ("the Great"; see entry). Alfred himself went to Rome as a small child, and was awed by the power of the church, the splendor of the city's imperial legacy, and the great wisdom passed down in Latin books from the writers of old.

Meanwhile, his homeland was in turmoil, thanks to a series of invasions by the Danes—one of the most prominent Viking groups—starting in 787. Young Alfred first made a name for himself in his early twenties, in 871, known as "the year of the battles." He scored a major triumph against the Danes at Ashdown, but lost his brother, King Ethelred, in another battle; subsequently the Witan, the Anglo-Saxon governing body, crowned Alfred king of Wessex.

Subsequent Danish victories forced Alfred to go into hiding. During this time, in an incident shrouded in legend, he went in disguise to a poor peasant's hut. The woman of the house, having no idea who he was, asked him to keep watch over some loaves of bread she was baking. Preoccupied by concerns for his country, Alfred let the loaves burn, and when the wife returned, she rebuked him sharply and

Though he was short, dressed poorly, and hardly spoke, a marriage of advantage could have been arranged with some other ruling house, and it would have been expected, because rulers in the Middle Ages placed a huge emphasis on fathering a son and successor. Basil's decision not to marry was particularly unfortunate, given the fact that none of his successors proved his equal: perhaps if he had had a son, he might have exerted greater influence on the next generation of leaders.

Bardas Sclerus and Bardas Phocas

A brilliant strategist and an extraordinarily capable leader, Basil spent most of his reign in the saddle, fighting a

King Alfred the Great.

boxed his ears. The next day, Alfred came in his royal clothes, attended by servants, to apologize to the woman.

In the struggle against the Danes, Alfred introduced two highly significant concepts: the militia, ancestor of citizen-soldier forces such as America's National Guard; and the first English navy. The latter was destined to become a powerful force in the nation's history through the twentieth century. Yet Alfred won peace with the Danes ultimately not through warfare, but through negotiation. He settled an agreement with a long-despised foe, the Dane's King Gutrum, whereby the northern part of England, the Danelaw, came under Danish control, while the Anglo-Saxons—with Alfred as their king—ruled the south.

With the Danish threat minimized, Alfred devoted much of his latter career to scholarship. He translated works of **Boethius**, Pope **Gregory I** (see entries), and the **Venerable Bede** (see entry on Historians) as well as the Bible, from Latin to the Old English spoken by the Anglo-Saxons.

number of conflicts. The first of these was an off-and-on conflict with two opposing men of influence, Bardas Sclerus and Bardas Phocas, each of whom intended to gain control over the empire. In line with its ancient Roman heritage, the Byzantine Empire did not recognize hereditary noblemen; but again like Rome itself, it had a powerful aristocratic class, to which both men belonged.

Each wanted to take the throne from Basil, and this conflict probably influenced his lifelong opposition to the Byzantine aristocracy. In 996, he would pass a law intended to simultaneously reduce the aristocrats' influence, gain the support of the poor, and fill the imperial coffers: according to this law, rich landlords were required to pay the taxes of the

Sundiata Keita

Like Basil II, Sundiata Keita (sun-JAH-tah kah-EE-tuh; died 1255), who was crippled at birth, came from unpromising beginnings. Yet he would grow up to establish the great empire of Mali, which would reach its height some years later under **Mansa Musa** (see entry).

Sundiata's family were rulers of a small West African kingdom called Kangaba, which they had controlled for about two centuries. They were constantly under threat from neighboring Kaniaga (kahn-ee-AH-guh), whose ruler in Sundiata's time was Sumanguru (sü-mahng-GÜ-roo). Sumanguru killed eleven of Sundiata's brothers, but did not consider the crippled Sundiata worth killing.

The Sundiata story is steeped in legend, making it hard to pick out the facts, but it appears that he was "miraculously" cured in his twenties, and was suddenly able to walk without difficulty. He soon distinguished himself as a hunter, and attracted a following of other young hunter-warriors. Meanwhile another surviving brother had become vassal king of Kangaba, subject to Sumanguru, and he considered Sundiata a threat. Sundiata finally had to go into exile, taking refuge with a king in nearby Mema (MAY-mah).

Ultimately the people of Kangaba became increasingly unhappy with the cruel system imposed on them by Sumanguru, and they finally revolted, forcing

local poor. In the meantime, during the late 980s, Basil found himself with his back against the wall, lacking support in his fight against the two would-be emperors. It was then that he hit on a brilliant idea.

Basil sent a message to the ruler of Kievan Russia, Vladimir (see box in St. Cyril and St. Methodius entry), informing him that if the Russians would provide him with six thousand soldiers, Basil would allow Vladimir to marry his sister. Marriage to a Byzantine princess, which would greatly improve his standing in the world, was exactly what Vladimir desired, and his support proved crucial to Basil's later victories. Bardas Phocas was defeated, and died in 989. Basil wisely allowed the blind and aging Bardas Sclerus to go free, and as a result gained the loyalty of the latter's many supporters.

Sundiata Keita. *Illustration by Moneta Barnett. Reproduced by permission of Doubleday.*

Sundiata's brother to flee. Seeing his chance, Sundiata formed an alliance with Mema and other states, and won control of Kangaba in 1234. He marched against Sumanguru in 1235, winning a great victory at Kirina on the Niger River—a bloody battle in which the hated Sumanguru lost his life.

The people of surrounding lands viewed Sundiata as a liberator, and thus he was able to spur them on to wars of conquest that expanded his realm in all directions. This led to the creation of Mali, an empire whose name means simply "where the king lives." Sundiata established his capital at Niani (nee-AHN-ee), which became renowned as a center of learning and trade.

Basil becomes the Bulgar-Slayer

Basil next turned his attention to the Bulgarians' King Samuel, who had earlier defeated him in a military engagement. From 990 to 994, he waged a series of brutal and successful campaigns against Samuel, but his attention was diverted by conflicts with the Muslim Fatimids in Egypt.

In 997, Samuel adopted the title *czar* or "caesar," which indicated that he had his eye on the Byzantine throne. This resulted in a third campaign that lasted from 998 to 1003, and once again Basil had to leave because of conflicts in the East. The Byzantines nonetheless managed to take some key cities, and after a decade they drove the Bulgarians to a last stand.

In 1014, Samuel sent some fifteen thousand men to defend an important mountain pass. Basil attacked from the rear, capturing about fourteen thousand soldiers, and he proceeded to deal them an extraordinarily harsh punishment. Byzantine soldiers blinded ninety-nine out of every 100 Bulgarian soldiers, leaving the last man with one good eye so that he could lead the others home. When Samuel saw the ghastly specter of his returning soldiers, he died of shock.

On to Armenia

Forever after known as the "Bulgar-Slayer," Basil incorporated Bulgarian lands into his empire, and set his attention on a land that had attracted Byzantine interest for many years: Armenia. Led by the Bagratid (bahg-RAH-teed) dynasty that also controlled nearby Georgia, the Armenians had united to resist Byzantine rule, and Basil responded by making a tactical withdrawal—that is, he took one step backward so that he could move forward by two steps. With the decline of the Fatimids, he regained territories in Syria and Iraq, and by 1001 was ready for the conquest of Armenia.

When he was not fighting the Bulgarians, Basil devoted much of his attention to conquering Armenia, a process that lasted beyond his lifetime. Byzantium was destined to control the country for only a short time, however: less than fifty years after Basil's death on December 15, 1025, the Seljuk Turks dealt the Byzantines a devastating blow at the Battle of Manzikert in 1071. This resulted in the Byzantines' loss of virtually all the lands Basil had gained, and sent the empire into a long, slow decay.

Yet Basil's legacy remained fixed, in part through his able administration of the empire, which along with his military victories brought Byzantium to its greatest glory since Justinian nearly five centuries before. He also influenced the Christianization of Russia, which would forever be tied to the Eastern Orthodox Church. At the time of his death, he was planning the reconquest of Sicily from the Arabs, and perhaps if his successors had been men of Basil's caliber, the empire's later history would have turned out to be quite different.

For More Information

Books

Chrisp, Peter. *The World of the Roman Emperor.* New York: P. Bedrick Books, 1999.

Corrick, James A. *The Byzantine Empire*. San Diego, CA: Lucent Books, 1997.

Davidson, Basil. *African Kingdoms*. Alexandria, VA: Time-Life Books, 1978.

Jenkins, Romilly. *Byzantium: The Imperial Centuries* A.D. *610–1071*. New York: Random House, 1966.

Johnson, Eleanor Noyes. *King Alfred the Great*. Illustrated by Arthur Wallower. Philadelphia: Westminster Press, 1966.

Mitchison, Naomi. *The Young Alfred the Great*. Illustrated by Shirley Farrow. New York: Roy Publishers, 1963.

Wisniewski, David. *Sundiata: Lion King of Mali*. Illustrations by the author. New York: Clarion Books, 1992.

Web Sites

"Alfred the Great." [Online] Available http://www.spartacus.schoolnet. co.uk/MEDalfred.htm (last accessed July 26, 2000).

"Background to the Epic of Sundiata Keita." [Online] Available http:// courses.wcupa.edu/jones/his311/notes/sundiata.htm (last accessed July 26, 2000).

"Byzantine and Medieval Web Links." *Medieval Sourcebook*. [Online] Available http://www.fordham.edu/halsall/medweb/links.htm (last accessed July 26, 2000).

"Mali—Formation of an Empire." [Online] Available http://xavier.xula. edu/~jrotondo/Kingdoms/Mali/Formation02.htm (last accessed July 26, 2000).

Bernard of Clairvaux

Born 1090
Died 1153

French monk and religious leader

Aside from royalty, politically influential figures of medieval Western Europe tended to be popes or other high church officials. Bernard of Clairvaux, by contrast, was a mere monk of the Cistercian order, and throughout his career held no official position of significance in the church—yet he was one of the most influential figures in the Catholic world.

In addition to his reform of the Cistercians, which he helped make one of the most powerful orders in Christendom, Bernard is remembered for his pivotal role in promoting the Second Crusade. When the latter ended in failure, he was widely criticized. He is also remembered with some disapproval as the man who tried to have **Abelard** (see entry) imprisoned for his unorthodox views. Yet he was also a figure of great sincerity, occasional compassion, and fascinating complexity.

Saving the Cistercian Order

Little is known about Bernard's life prior to the time he joined the Cistercian (sis-TUR-shun) order. An order is an

"Men are saying it is not you but I who am the Pope, and from all sides they are flocking to me."

Letter to Pope Eugenius III, a former student

Portrait: *Reproduced by permission of Archive Photos, Inc.*

organized religious community within the Catholic Church, and the Cistercians were monks who sought out a particularly austere, or hard, lifestyle. They did this because they believed that only by denying the needs of the physical body could they truly concentrate on God.

The life of a Cistercian was not for everyone, and though it had only been founded in 1098, its numbers were dwindling when Bernard joined twelve years later. Twenty-year-old Bernard arrived at the Cistercians' abbey in the French town of Citeaux (see-TOH; hence the name Cistercian) with great religious zeal. Like a military recruit who opts for the marines or special forces in the other armed services, he was eager to be tested, and courted the challenges of the Cistercian way of life. So great was his enthusiasm, in fact, that he brought with him thirty male friends and relatives he had convinced to join him. In so doing, he saved the entire Cistercian movement, which at that point consisted of only thirteen members.

The Cistercians quite literally gave Bernard the name by which he is known. When the abbot at Citeaux saw how Bernard had saved the monastery there, he appointed him to establish a second one at Clairvaux (klayr-VOH) some seventy miles away. By the end of Bernard's life, the Cistercians would claim not one or two, but 340 monasteries, and much of the credit belongs to him.

Bernard v. Abelard

Bernard was clearly a strong-willed person, and he had very definite ideas about religious faith. In a dozen books and many hundreds of letters, he addressed a variety of issues, but always with one or two central themes. In Bernard's view, religious meditation—one of the principal activities of a monk's life—was better than action. Action, in his mind, was an example of man's will, whereas contemplation and meditation forced the believer to submit to God's will. He also maintained that religious faith was infinitely superior to intellectual, or mental, reasoning power. Once again, it was a matter of submitting to God rather than trusting in one's own strength.

In his zeal, Bernard worked to promote his ideas through his writings, and this ironically forced him to leave

Shem Tov ibn Shem Tov and His Family

Bernard of Clairvaux is remembered, along with his many achievements, for his reaction to the efforts of Abelard and others to reconcile religious belief on the one hand and reasoning ability on the other. Catholics such as Bernard were not the only religious believers likely to oppose such efforts to understand faith: many Muslims were slow to accept the ideas of thinkers such as **Averroës** (see entry) and Avicenna (see box in Moses Maimonides entry), who made a similar attempt to bring together the worlds of faith and reason. **Moses Maimonides** (see entry) also tried to find a balance between the life of the spirit and the life of the mind—and he too found opposition among fellow Jews.

An interesting case in point is Shem Tov ibn Shem Tov (TAWV; c. 1380–c. 1441) and his son and grandson. ("Ibn" and "ben" are, respectively, Arabic and Hebrew titles meaning "son of." Shem Tov and his descendants each added a "ben" or "ibn" to their father's names, meaning that their names grew progressively longer.)

Shem Tov was a cabalist, an adherent of the cabala (kuh-BAH-luh; also *kabbala* and *qabala*). The latter is a mystical Jewish belief system based on the idea that every single word—and letter, and number, and even accent mark in Hebrew—of the Jewish scriptures has a specific meaning. To cabalists, the word of God is filled with a sort of secret code that is extremely difficult to grasp and can be revealed only by spiritual means rather than by intellectual or mental effort.

Given these beliefs, it is not surprising that Shem Tov was vehemently opposed to Maimonides's reliance on the teachings of the ancient Greek philosopher Aristotle, who believed that all knowledge can be perceived through the mind. But there was a sort of generation gap in Shem Tov's family, because his son Joseph ben Shem Tov ibn Shem Tov (c. 1400–c. 1460) took a much friendlier approach toward the work of Maimonides, Aristotle, and others. A court physician in Castile, Spain, Joseph attempted to draw parallels between philosophy and religion, and in particular compared Aristotle's ideas with those of the Jewish scriptures.

By the time of Joseph's son Shem Tov ben Joseph ben Shem Tov ibn Shem Tov (flourished 1461–1489), attitudes in Shem Tov's family had undergone a 180-degree shift. This third-generation Shem Tov was an admirer of Maimonides, and wrote commentaries on Averroës as well. By the grandson's time, of course, the Middle Ages were drawing to a close, and viewpoints were beginning to change.

behind the life of meditation he valued. He soon became a prominent spokesman for the church, a defender of the faith as he saw it. In the late 1130s, he engaged in his infamous conflict with Abelard, whose teachings challenged established church beliefs. To a modern person, Abelard's ideas, such as his position that reason has a place in religion—that it is possible both to think and to believe—hardly seem controversial; but that was not so in the twelfth century.

Bernard was not the only person who saw Abelard as a danger, but he was certainly the most eloquent spokesperson for the church in the matter. For several years, Bernard and Abelard conducted a heated public argument, rather like two boxers in a shouting match before the big fight. The showdown finally came in June 1140, when the two were supposed to engage in a public debate. But the sides were hardly matched: Bernard represented the power of the church—which in the Middle Ages could call on the police force and legal system to do its bidding—whereas Abelard was merely a brilliant scholar with a strong student following.

On the other hand, Bernard was intimidated by Abelard's nimble skill at argumentation, and he had no intention of engaging in a debate with him. Therefore he arrived at the meeting prepared to put Abelard on trial for heresy, or beliefs that went against the teachings of the church. Given the situation, Abelard had no choice but to back down.

The Second Crusade

Bernard's power and influence continued to rise, particularly when in 1145 a former monk who had studied under him at Clairvaux became Pope Eugenius III. This made Eugenius, as head of the Catholic Church, the most powerful man in Western Europe—but since he took Bernard's advice on many matters, it was debatable who actually held more power.

In 1146, Eugenius called upon Bernard's help in a matter of great importance. Half a century earlier, the Catholic nations of Europe had mobilized for the First Crusade (1095–99), in which they seized control of the Holy Land from the Muslims. Now they had lost their stronghold at Edessa near Jerusalem, and the pope wanted to launch a new crusade. Bernard, at first reluctant, finally agreed to preach a crusading sermon at Palm Sunday—the beginning of Easter week, the most important time of year for Christians.

The response to Bernard's message—he preached more such sermons, and sent out letters promoting the proposed crusade—was overwhelming. Some of that response, however, was unwelcome. One of the most awful aspects of the First Crusade was its unexpected arousal of anti-Semitic attacks in which many Jews were killed and many others lost all their property. The dawning of a new crusade brought with it a new wave of anti-Jewish hatred, and among its leading proponents was a German Cistercian named Rudolph. Bernard denounced Rudolph, pointing out that Jesus Christ himself was a Jew.

The crusade turned out to be a disaster, and in the aftermath Bernard, who had earlier been celebrated, became the target of blame. Despite the failed project, Bernard continued to believe in the crusading ideal. He actively supported the Knights Templars, a group of warriors who claimed to be soldiers for Christ. In fact many Templars joined the group simply for personal gain, and often their behavior was savage.

Bernard of Clairvaux was the object of harsh criticism after the Second Crusade, which he had promoted, proved to be a disaster. *Reproduced by permission of the Library of Congress.*

The admiration of foes

Bernard behaved in an underhanded way on two notable occasions: in the proposed debate with Abelard, and later in a similar situation with another opponent. For the most part, however, it could be said that while he may have been many things, he was neither dishonest nor insincere. He also tended to think that others would act the same, and thus could not understand, for instance, that someone might go on a crusade for a reason other than to do God's will.

Despite his shortcomings, he was widely admired, and after his death in 1153, followers claimed to have experienced a number of miracles around the site of his grave. But perhaps the greatest testimony came from men whom Bernard would undoubtedly have considered enemies: Martin Luther and John Calvin, sixteenth-century leaders of the Reformation, in which Protestant denominations broke away from Bernard's beloved Catholic Church. Despite those differences of belief, Luther praised Bernard, and Calvin said of him, "the Abbot Bernard speaks in the language of the truth itself."

For More Information

Books

Abrahams, Israel. *Jewish Life in the Middle Ages*. Philadelphia: Jewish Publication Society, 1993.

Bruno, James. *St. Bernard of Clairvaux*. New York: Harper, 1959.

Metford, J. C. *Dictionary of Christian Lore and Legend*. London: Thames & Hudson, 1983.

Runciman, Steven. *A History of the Crusades*. New York: Cambridge University Press, 1954.

Schmid, Evan. *The Mighty Bernard: A Story of St. Bernard of Clairvaux*. Notre Dame, IN: Dujarie Press, 1959.

Web Sites

"CIN—St. Bernard of Clairvaux." [Online] Available http://www.cin.org/saints/bernclai.html (last accessed July 26, 2000).

"OSB. The Cistercians and the Trappists. Index." *Order of Saint Benedict.* [Online] Available http://www.osb.org/cist/ (last accessed July 26, 2000).

Pennington, M. Basil, O.C.S.O. "The Cistercians." [Online] Available http://www2.csbsju.edu/osb/cist/bern.html (last accessed July 26, 2000).

Boethius

Born 480
Died 524

Roman philosopher

In his *Consolation of Philosophy,* written in a prison cell as he awaited execution, Boethius developed a view of the world that came to symbolize the medieval age in Europe. True virtue, he explained, lay not in changing one's fate, but in accepting the fate one was assigned by Fortune. His personification of "Fortune" and "Philosophy" as women also set the tone for countless medieval allegories, symbolic stories in which characters represented ideas. Though he was born after the fall of the Western Roman Empire, Boethius was a Roman to the core, and as with **Augustine** (see entry), his writings represent a vital link between the ancient and medieval worlds.

> "In all adversity of fortune, it is the most unhappy kind of misfortune to have been happy."
>
> *From* The Consolation of Philosophy

A distinguished Roman family

Four years before Boethius (boh-EE-thee-us) was born, the Western Roman Empire came to an end when the Germanic chieftain Odoacer (oh-doh-AY-sur; c. 433–493) removed the last Roman emperor from power and declared himself "king of Italy." At the time, people did not perceive the fall of the Roman Empire as an earth-shattering event,

Boethius, with a woman who is intended to represent the human embodiment of Philosophy. *Reproduced by permission of the Corbis Corporation.*

one which many historians regard as the beginning of the Middle Ages. For one thing, there still was a Roman Empire—only it was the Eastern Roman Empire, based in Greece and referred to by modern scholars as the Byzantine Empire.

Though in fact he ruled Italy as a separate kingdom, Odoacer had declared himself a servant of the Eastern Roman emperor, and many Romans believed that business would continue as usual. Certainly that was the impression among Boethius's family, a distinguished line that could trace their roots back more than six centuries. Several of his relatives, along with other leading Roman citizens, served Odoacer in important positions.

Education for leadership

Before he reached his teens, Boethius, whose full name was Anicius Manlius Severinus Boethius, lost his father. Therefore another prominent Roman named Symmachus (SIM-uh-kus) became his guardian, and looked after his education. Boethius's generation was one of the last to enjoy the full range of learning from Greece, which had been expanded by the writings of great Roman figures.

In the course of his education, he was exposed to the writings of Plato (PLAY-toh; 427–347 B.C.), whose *Republic* offered a model for participation in government by philosophers, or men who devoted their time to contemplating the deepest questions of existence. Plato was one of the greatest of the ancient Greek philosophers, and his ideas were to have an effect on Boethius throughout his life.

Not only was he fluent in Greek, but Boethius also wrote in a classical form of Latin. The latter language would continue to survive during the Middle Ages, but in a different form; the Latin that Boethius knew was more closely linked to that of the Roman Empire's golden age centuries before than it was to the Latin used by Europeans just a few decades after his time. Boethius, however, had no idea that the world of classical Rome was fading so rapidly: in his mind, his education was training for leadership, after which he would take a prominent role, as members of his family had done for centuries.

A flourishing career

A good marriage—that is, marriage to someone of equal or higher social rank—was essential to the career of a noble Roman. Thus Boethius was married to Symmachus's daughter Rusticana, with whom he had two sons. Years later, in his prison cell, he would look back on the joy he had shared with his family, and this only added to his sorrow. Hence his statement that "in all adversity of fortune, it is the most unhappy kind of misfortune to have been happy."

Boethius rose through the ranks, reaching the position of consul in 510. Centuries earlier, under the Roman Republic (507–31 B.C.), the city's two consuls had ruled not only Rome, but all of its territorial possessions as well. Times had changed, however, and Rome was no longer even the capital of Italy. The government had moved to the city of Ravenna, where a new king was in charge: Theodoric (c. 454–526), an Ostrogoth or eastern Goth chieftain who had slain Odoacer.

Theodoric was to have a tragic effect on Boethius's career, but that still lay in the future as Boethius busied himself with his political duties and his studies. The former included service in the senate, the body that had governed Rome for a thousand years. As for his studies, these included the topics of the quadrivium, a group of four subjects studied by Romans for ages: arithmetic, music, geometry, and astronomy. Boethius wrote considerably on these and other subjects.

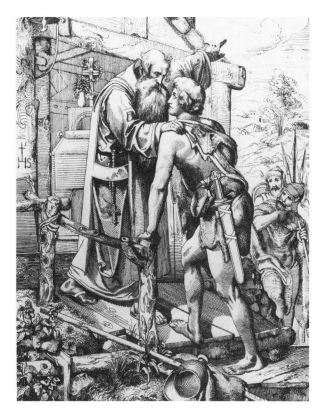

Odoacer (right; listening to the hermit Severin) was a Germanic chieftain who removed the Roman emperor from power and declared himself king of Italy in 476. Though people did not realize the importance of this event at the time, Odoacer's takeover marked the end of the Western Roman Empire. *Reproduced by permission of the Corbis Corporation.*

Trouble with the authorities

He would not have long to enjoy the privileges of his birth, because events soon took place that would ultimately bring about the end of his life. Troubled by corruption, long

Ashikaga Takauji

In viewing the Middle Ages, it would be hard to find two individuals more different than Boethius and Ashikaga Takauji (tah-kah-OO-jee; 1305–1358), who founded a dynasty of Japanese *shoguns,* or military leaders. The comparison is worthwhile because both men were members of their countries' noble classes; but whereas Boethius was accused of treason in his lifetime and was believed innocent by later generations, Ashikaga is remembered as, among other things, a traitor. Furthermore, Boethius's life was defined by his ability to suffer injustice in silence, whereas Ashikaga took action against what he considered an unjust situation.

This contrast is particularly interesting in light of what many people believe about Western civilization, of which Boethius was a part, in contrast to the Eastern civilizations of Japan, China, India, and other countries. According to this line of thought, the Eastern tradition is characterized by silent submission to one's fate, whereas the West is more associated with the idea of taking action to correct perceived wrongs. In the case of Boethius and Ashikaga, exactly the opposite was true.

Though Japan was formally under the control of an emperor, the real power lay in prominent families such as the Kamakura, who established the first of two shogunates that were to control the country off and on between 1192 and 1573. Ashikaga founded the second of these shogunates, but not before he helped bring down the Kamakura in a somewhat underhanded way.

Typically, Japanese emperors were children who were easily manipulated by the shoguns and powerful families, but in 1318, a full-grown adult named Go-Daigo

a factor in the Roman government, Boethius made enemies in high places when he tried to protect honest men from attacks by greedy and power-hungry leaders.

His real misfortune began, however, in 522, when he came to the defense of a senator accused of treason. It appears that Boethius may have thought the senator guilty, but he wanted to protect the reputation of the senate, and this exposed him to charges of suppressing evidence. He was then accused of aiding Justin I, the Byzantine emperor, against Theodoric. Therefore Theodoric ordered that he be imprisoned in the town of Pavia (PAHV-ee-uh).

(goh DY-goh; 1288–1339) assumed the throne. When Go-Daigo revolted against the shoguns, they exiled him in 1331, but he escaped two years later. The leaders trusted Ashikaga to capture him, but in the process of doing so, Ashikaga made a deal with Go-Daigo.

Claiming to be a secret supporter of the emperor, Ashikaga joined forces with him to overthrow the Hojo family, who had assumed control of the Kamakura shogunate. Once Go-Daigo was restored to power, however, he proved an inept ruler, and offended Ashikaga by appointing his son, rather than Ashikaga himself, as shogun. In 1336, Ashikaga ousted Go-Daigo, and replaced him with an emperor who appointed him to the all-important shogun position.

Thus was born the Ashikaga shogunate (1338–1573), sometimes referred to as the Muromachi period because its cultural life centered on the Muromachi district of Tokyo. And indeed it was a time of cultural flourishing, for which Ashikaga deserves much of the credit. His place in Japanese history is somewhat uncertain, however, due in part to the fact that many scholars believe he was overshadowed by his powerful grandson Yoshimitsu (ruled 1368–95).

A greater source of controversy regarding Ashikaga, however, relates to what many consider his treacherous actions. In that vein, he is often compared unfavorably to Kusunoki Masashige (mah-sah-SHEE-gay; 1294–1336), a warlord who remained faithful to Go-Daigo and committed suicide after he was defeated by Ashikaga. Regardless of his moral stature, however, Ashikaga was undoubtedly a brilliant strategist and leader who ushered in a culturally significant era of Japanese history.

The Consolation of Philosophy

Boethius would spend the remaining two years of his life in jail, where he wrote his most enduring work, *The Consolation of Philosophy*. He had written a number of books before, but without the *Consolation* his name might well have been forgotten. As it was, he set the tone for a thousand years of European history.

Though he was a devout Christian, the *Consolation* is a work of philosophy and makes little direct reference to Christian principles. Its message that suffering should be endured might seem to bear a close relation to the teachings of Christ,

Theodoric, an Ostrogoth chieftain who came to rule Italy after killing Odoacer, imprisoned Boethius, accusing him of supporting Theodoric's rival, Byzantine emperor Justin I. *Reproduced by permission of Archive Photos, Inc.*

but Christ taught that believers in God should endure suffering with the hope of a reward in Heaven. The *Consolation*, by contrast, seems to say that suffering is its own reward, and in this it is more closely tied to the ancient Roman tradition of Stoicism (STOH-uh-sizm), which held that true nobility is found in withstanding hardship.

Nonetheless, the message that "Lady Philosophy" delivers to Boethius—the book is built around the idea that the spirit of philosophy came to visit him in his cell, clothed in the body of an otherworldly woman—has an underlying Christian theme. By the end of the work, Philosophy shows him that God's justice can be seen even in the most random and arbitrary-seeming misfortune. Furthermore, she shows him that although man has free will to choose good or evil (a central belief of Christianity), true freedom lies in choosing virtue.

Echoes of Boethius

Boethius died in prison in 524, either by execution or as the result of torture. He quickly came to be regarded as a martyr, or someone who dies for their faith, though in fact he died for his convictions about morality and politics. Nonetheless, he was declared a saint, and he had an enduring effect on medieval thought.

Much of that effect may be judged as unfortunate from the viewpoint of a modern person: by teaching people to accept their fate, one might reason, Boethius was condemning them to unnecessary suffering. But to take that approach is to view Boethius from the perspective of the present, rather than from that of the sixth century.

Among Boethius's many admirers were the ninth-century Anglo-Saxon king Alfred the Great (see box in Basil II entry) and the sixteenth-century English queen Elizabeth I, both of whom produced translations of *The Consolation of Philosophy.* Esteemed by figures such as **Dante** (see entry) and the English writer **Geoffrey Chaucer** (see English Scholars, Thinkers, and Writers entry), he continued to exert an influence almost a millennium after his death.

For More Information

Books

Chadwick, Henry. *Boethius: The Consolations of Music, Logic, Theology, and Philosophy.* Oxford, England: Clarendon Press, 1981.

Encyclopedia of World Biography, second edition. Detroit: Gale, 1998.

Historic World Leaders. Detroit: Gale, 1994.

Web Sites

Boethius. [Online] Available http://www.smcm.edu/users/bsthomassen/boethius.html (last accessed July 26, 2000).

"Boethius." [Online] Available http://ccat.sas.upenn.edu/jod/boethius.html (last accessed July 26, 2000).

"Boethius." [Online] Available http://www.wsu.edu:8000/~dee/CHRIST/BOETHIUS.HTM (last accessed July 26, 2000).

"Japan in the Ashikaga, Sengoku, and Tokugawa Eras." [Online] Available http://www.loyno.edu/~history/worldciv/ppoint/toku/sld001.htm (last accessed July 26, 2000).

Charlemagne

Born 742
Died 814

Frankish king and emperor of the West

Charlemagne was unquestionably the most important ruler in Western Europe between 400 and 1000. Only **Clovis** (see entry) could compete for that distinction, but Charlemagne—who like Clovis came from the nation called the Franks—achieved far more than Clovis could even have imagined. In Clovis's time the Franks, one of many tribes that invaded former Roman territories, conquered much of what is now France, in the process giving their name to the country; Charlemagne's power, by contrast, would extend throughout the entire western portion of the European continent.

Yet Charlemagne's impact went far beyond the military victories that built his vast empire. By forging an alliance with the church, he solidified the idea of kings and popes as joint political leaders. Furthermore, by encouraging the arts and scholarship, he fostered a rebirth of learning in the West.

Merovingians and Carolingians

When Charlemagne (SHAR-luh-mayn) was born, France was under the rule of the Merovingian (mayr-uh-VIN-jee-un) dynasty or royal house, whose power Clovis had established nearly three centuries before. But later Merovingians had proven to be weak rulers, and were dominated by palace officials called majordomos, or "mayors of the palace." The greatest of the majordomos was Charlemagne's grandfather, Charles Martel (known as "The Hammer," c. 688–741), who was clearly the real power in Merovingian France.

When Charles died, his son Pepin III (c. 714–768) decided to take the throne, and in 751 sent a message to the pope, spiritual leader of western Christianity, asking if it would be a sin to remove the Merovingian king from power. The pope, who needed Pepin's help to defend Italy against an invading tribe called the Lombards, gave his blessing, whereupon Pepin seized the throne. Thus he began a new dynasty, which historians call the Carolingian (kayr-uh-LINJ-ee-un) in honor of its greatest ruler, Pepin's son Charlemagne.

Training for kingship

Actually, he only became known as Charlemagne, or "Charles the Great," much later: in his boyhood he had simply been known as Charles. At the time Pepin took power, Charlemagne was only nine years old, and in that same year, his younger brother Carloman was born. Pepin raised both boys to succeed him, since it was the Frankish custom for a king to divide his lands between his sons.

No doubt part of Charlemagne's education involved training in the arts of war, which he practiced by riding and hunting. He did not learn how to read and write, since at that time only priests and other members of the church acquired such skills. Later in life, Charlemagne attempted to teach himself reading and writing, but it is doubtful that he ever became fully literate. Nonetheless, he received a valuable education in kingly skills by accompanying his father on several trips around France.

Certainly he looked like a king. Famed for his piercing blue eyes, Charlemagne as an adult was a giant, standing six feet, four inches at a time when most men were a foot shorter. He was also a devout Christian, and when he started a family, a loving father.

In 768, when Charlemagne was twenty-six, Pepin died, leaving Charlemagne and Carloman as joint rulers. Three years later Carloman—with whom Charlemagne was not close—died, leaving Charlemagne as sole ruler of the Franks.

A series of wars

Charlemagne spent the early years of his reign in an almost constant state of war. In 772, his forces went to war against the Saxons, a Germanic tribe to the north of France. The Saxons were pagans, meaning that they worshiped many gods, and in his first campaign against them, Charlemagne chopped down a tree that they considered a sacred symbol of their religion.

Between 773 and 776, he did battle with the Lombards, subduing northern Italy. He then turned his attention to Spain, which was under the control of Islamic or Muslim forces from the Middle East. Though the Muslims defeated Charlemagne's forces in 778, the campaign was memorable because it served as the basis for the *Song of Roland*, a twelfth-century French legend.

In 781, Charlemagne had his son Pepin crowned king of Italy by the pope, and in the following year he increased the intensity of his ten-year-old campaign against the Saxons. A rebellion led to a stern punishment by Charlemagne, whose soldiers beheaded some five thousand Saxons. Meanwhile, he continued his campaign in Italy, and by 786 had gained control of the entire Italian peninsula.

The Carolingian Renaissance

Despite his preoccupation with military matters, Charlemagne was also highly interested in education and set about to foster scholarship throughout his empire. Thus in the 780s he ushered in a period sometimes referred to as the "Carolingian Renaissance" (RIN-uh-sahnts), the latter term referring to a rebirth of learning.

Charlemagne achieved this renaissance by inviting to France scholars from various parts of Western Europe, most notably **Alcuin** (AL-kwin; c. 735–804; see English Scholars, Thinkers, and Writers entry) from England. Alcuin called for a return to the study of Latin, and to standards of education

Charlemagne is considered the most important Western European ruler of the Middle Ages. *Reproduced by permission of the Corbis Corporation.*

that had prevailed under the Greek and Roman civilizations. He directed a school at Charlemagne's palace, a training ground for young men who would later work in the government. Another important scholar in Carolingian France was Charlemagne's secretary, Einhard (c. 770–840), whose *Life of Charlemagne* is one of the principal sources of information about the king.

Before the invention of the printing press, books had to be copied by hand, and more than ninety percent of the works from ancient Rome that exist today owe their survival to Carolingian monks. The originals of such books have long since disappeared, and without the Carolingians, who copied them, no one would know of these writings. Furthermore, much of the lettering system used today—Roman script (best known through the Times Roman font on most computer printers), italics, even lowercase lettering—owes its existence to the monks of Carolingian France.

Architecture also flourished under Charlemagne. The emperor was so impressed by the Church of San Vitale at Ravenna in Italy, built after **Justinian** (see entry) conquered that country, that he was determined to have his own version. The result was the chapel at Aachen (AH-kin), a city in what is now western Germany that Charlemagne designated as his capital in 794. Charlemagne's architect, Odo of Metz, designed a highly distinctive building rather than an imitation, and the chapel served as a model for later styles of architecture in Western Europe.

Emperor of the Romans

The establishment of a permanent capital was an achievement in itself, since medieval kings tended to move from place to place. The Carolingian age signified the beginning of a return to the civilized way of life that had prevailed before the fall of the Western Roman Empire in 476, and in 800, Charlemagne received a title that recognized him as the leader of a new Roman Empire.

The year before, Pope Leo III had been attacked by mobs in Rome and imprisoned. He had escaped and gone to Aachen for help, and Charlemagne had assisted him with a contingent of soldiers. Soon they restored the pope to power,

and Charlemagne himself came to Rome in mid-December 800. On Christmas Day, the pope placed a crown on his head and declared him "Emperor of the Romans." Historians regard this as an early foundation for the Holy Roman Empire, which would take shape nearly two centuries later.

Though this empire was more of an idea than a reality, it would still play a significant part in European politics throughout the remainder of the Middle Ages. Certainly the Byzantine emperors, who ruled the Eastern Roman Empire from Greece, took the title seriously enough that they regarded it as an insult to their own claims to the Roman throne. Only in 813 did they recognize Charlemagne's use of the title.

The legacy of Charlemagne

The coronation of Charlemagne was the high point of his career. He devoted the remaining fourteen years of his life

Though much of Charlemagne's reign was spent in military pursuits, he also surrounded himself with thinkers and educators and fostered a rebirth of learning in his kingdom.
Reproduced by permission of the Corbis Corporation.

The Palatine Chapel in Aachen, Charlemagne's capital, was the site of the crowning of his successor, his son Louis the Pious, in 813. *Reproduced by permission of the Corbis Corporation.*

to the administration of his empire rather than to the conquest of new territory, and he spent most of his time in Aachen, which was famed for its soothing mineral baths. In 806, he started making arrangements to pass his lands on to his three sons, but by 813, only one was still living. Therefore in a magnificent ceremony at Aachen, he placed the crown on the head of his son Louis the Pious. On January 21, 814, following a bath in the mineral springs, Charlemagne developed a sudden fever and died a week later.

His empire did not last long: in the Treaty of Verdun (843), Louis divided it between his three sons, and it gradually fell apart. Descendants of Charlemagne ruled France until 887, and parts of Germany until 911. The idea of a unified western empire, however, was a powerful one, and later Otto the Great (912–973) would revive the concept when he founded the Holy Roman Empire. A later Holy Roman emperor, Frederick I Barbarossa (ruled 1152–90) had Charlemagne canonized, or declared a saint.

For More Information

Books

Biel, Timothy L. *Charlemagne.* San Diego, CA: Lucent Books, 1997.

MacDonald, Fiona. *The World in the Time of Charlemagne.* Parsippany, NJ: Dillon Press, 1998.

Pollard, Michael. *Absolute Rulers.* Ada, OK: Garrett, 1992.

Price-Groff, Claire. *Great Conquerors.* San Diego, CA: Lucent Books, 2000.

Motion Pictures

Charlemagne (television). Pathe Television, 1994.

Web Sites

"Charlemagne: Founder of the Holy Roman Empire." [Online] Available http://www.ptialaska.net/~airloom/charlema.htm (last accessed July 26, 2000).

"Charlemagne: King of the Franks." [Online] Available http://www2.lucidcafe.com/lucidcafe/library/96apr/charlemagne.html (last accessed July 26, 2000).

"Charlemagne Links." [Online] Available http://pages.prodigy.com/charlemagne/links.htm (last accessed July 26, 2000).

Imperium. [Online] Available http://www.ghgcorp.com/shetler/oldimp/ (last accessed July 26, 2000).

Christine de Pisan

Born c. 1364
Died c. 1430

French poet and essayist

Christine de Pisan was the first known woman in Europe to earn her living by writing. As a poet, she won much acclaim among the nobility of France and neighboring lands. Her extensive essays and works of scholarship, most notably *The City of Ladies,* provide a valuable contribution to an understanding not only of her own ideas, but also of European society during the Middle Ages.

Christine was a true feminist who used her pen to make the case that women should enjoy the same rights before God as men. She did not undertake her poetic work or other writings out of lofty ideals, or as a hobby; rather, she wrote because she had to support her family.

In the court of Charles V

Christine de Pisan (pee-ZAHN; sometimes rendered as Pizan) was born in the Italian city of Venice in 1364. Her father, Tommaso di Benvenuto da Pizzano, was a professor of astrology at the university of Bologna (buh-LOHN-yuh),

"I am alone and I want to be alone."

Line from a poem written after her husband's death, on her decision not to remarry

Portrait: *Photograph by Gianni Dagli Orti. Reproduced by permission of the Corbis Corporation.*

69

another Italian city. Astrology is a system that attempts to show that a person's destiny is influenced by the position of the stars and planets at the time of her birth, and though it has long since been discredited as a science, medieval people held it in high regard. Accordingly, Tommaso received two highly attractive invitations soon after Christine's birth: he could serve either in the court of the Hungarian king or that of the French king, Charles V. He opted to go to Paris, the French capital, which was noted for its outstanding university.

After a year in France without his family, Thomas de Pisan, as he was now called in the French style, agreed to stay on as court astrologer, alchemist (practitioner of another medieval non-science based on the belief that plain metals such as iron could be turned into gold), and physician. He therefore sent for his family, and his wife and four-year-old daughter joined him. Christine therefore had an opportunity to grow up amid the lively atmosphere of the court presided over by Charles, who was nicknamed "the Wise." Her father saw to her education, and she learned to read and write, something usually taught only to girls in the highest levels of medieval society.

Marriage, children, and tragedy

When she was fifteen years old, Christine married Étienne (ey-TYAn) du Castel, a scholar nine years her senior. Theirs was a happy marriage that produced three children. The second child, a son, died in infancy; the first child, a daughter, later became a nun. The last child, a son named Jean (ZHAWn), born when Christine was twenty-one, grew up to serve in the court of the duke of Burgundy.

Beginning in 1380, when she was sixteen, a series of tragedies struck Christine's life. First Charles V died, and Christine's father was dismissed from his position at court. A few years later, her father became ill and died in poverty. In 1389 Étienne succumbed to the plague, an epidemic disease that periodically struck Europe throughout the Middle Ages. Christine was left without a father or a husband—and with two children to support.

Queen Margaret of Denmark

It is interesting to note that the birth and death dates of Western Europe's first female professional writer, Christine de Pisan (c. 1364–c. 1430) correspond closely with those of its first ruling woman monarch, Queen Margaret of Denmark (1353–1412). Over the course of her career, Margaret united her homeland with Norway and Sweden, the two other principal nations of Scandinavia, to form the largest single political entity in Europe at the time.

Scandinavia had long before ceased to be the homeland of the much-feared Vikings, and in their place were several kingdoms divided by politics and language. The mid-1300s saw an incredibly complex series of maneuvers to determine which royal house would control the area, and an alliance of German cities known as the Hanseatic League tried to exert its influence. When she was ten, Margaret's father Valdemar IV arranged her marriage to King Haakon (HAH-kohn) VI of Norway.

Valdemar died without a male heir in 1375, and Margaret's only child Olaf became king. Five years later, Haakon died as well, and Margaret arranged for Olaf to succeed to the Norwegian throne. Then in

Queen Margaret. *Reproduced by permission of the Library of Congress.*

1387, Olaf died, and after a power struggle with another claimant to the Swedish throne, Margaret became queen of all three lands in 1389. In 1400 she designated an heir, her great-nephew Erik, but she continued to control affairs until her death twelve years later. Though she was often criticized for her harsh policies, Margaret was able to forge an alliance of all three Scandinavian lands. The union with Sweden would last for more than a century, and the one with Norway until 1814.

Forced to write

As with **Murasaki Shikibu** (see entry), the world's first novelist (and also a woman), Christine was forced into her career through personal tragedy. Unlike Murasaki, however, she did not write simply to console herself in her loss, though that was certainly a factor. Primarily, however, she turned to the vocation of writing, at which she had earlier displayed a talent, in order to feed her family.

Later Christine would recount how, at age twenty-five, she was forced to take on "the role of a man." In medieval Europe, women were not supposed to be breadwinners, but she had little choice: though her husband had left behind a small inheritance, it became tied up in legal battles, and she did not see any money from it for a decade. Yet she was determined to support herself, rather than seek out a marriage to someone she did not love simply as a means of paying the bills: hence a famous line from a poem written after her husband's death: "Seulete suy et seulete vueil estre" (I am alone and I want to be alone).

First mature writings

At that time, the most popular type of literature in Western Europe was courtly love poetry, which dealt with themes of idealized romance. Christine disagreed with many of the principles behind such poetry, as she would later reveal, but she had to write material for a buying audience. In modern times, a writer sells his or her work to a publisher, who distributes it to a wide public; but in the medieval world, there simply was no wide reading public. A writer such as Christine composed her verses for nobility and royalty, who acted as her patrons, financially supporting her work.

Christine soon broadened her output to include short narratives or stories, and didactic works, or writings meant to instruct. The latter was another popular format in medieval times, an era that saw the beginnings of what modern people would call "self-help" literature. One type of didactic writing, for instance, was the courtesy book, a sort of how-to manual for people who wanted to learn how to behave around the higher classes of society. She augmented her writing with an extensive program of study, and by the turn of the fourteenth century, when she was about thirty-five, she began to write the first of her more mature works.

Among these were works such as *The Book of Changes in Fortune* (1400–3), in which she questioned the power of fate to alter human affairs, as it had her own. Using a practice common to many medieval writers, she represented Fortune as a Roman goddess, and examined Fortune's effect on events throughout history. Another work from this period was *The Book of the Road of Long Study* (1402–3), which was an allegorical piece along the lines of the *Divine Comedy* by **Dante** (see entry)—in other words, it used characters and actions to illustrate ideas. Both books achieved wide acclaim, and therefore King Charles VI commissioned her to write a biography of his predecessor, which became *The Book of the Deeds and Virtues of the Wise King Charles V* (1404).

Christine's feminism

Another allegorical work of the Middle Ages that attracted widespread attention was the thirteenth-century *Romance of the Rose,* which portrayed a man's love for a woman as a difficult and almost unrewarding quest. Christine, who took issue with the portrayal of women in the *Romance,* was moved to write several pieces as a response. Among these was *The Epistle to the God of Love* (1399), in which Cupid becomes so disgusted with men's mistreatment of women that he forbids all men in his court from saying bad things about them.

For some time, Christine had been feeling the stirrings of what might be called feminism, a desire to stand up for women's rights. Of course "feminism" is a modern idea, and Christine had no concept of issues that concern feminists today—for instance, women receiving less pay for doing the same job as a man. Her appeals regarding treatment of women began with a critique of how they were portrayed in literature. She had stopped writing courtly love poetry, she said, because she came to see it as poetry written to make men feel better about mistreating women. The ideal of courtly love, reduced to its essentials, involved a man and woman who were not married to one another, but who shared a romantic and usually sexual relationship: thus the man got what he wanted without having to make a commitment.

The Book of the City of Ladies

Though Christine also wrote *The Tale of the Rose* (1401) and *Epistles on the Romance of the Rose* (1401–2), her most celebrated response to the *Romance*—and indeed her most well known work—was *The Book of the City of Ladies* (1404–5). The latter asks why misogyny (mi-SAHJ-uh-nee; hatred of women) has been such a popular theme throughout history. In the narrative, the author suggests that it is because men have controlled the writing of works about women, and in an allegorical tale she describes how she became depressed by this realization.

At that point, she explains, Reason, Justice, and Righteousness appeared to her in the form of three crowned ladies and commissioned her to establish a "city of ladies." The idea of this "city" is a clear reference to **Augustine**'s (see entry) *City of God,* indicating that she saw her city within the context of the Christian faith. She pointed to a number of passages in the Bible indicating that God had given men and women the same spiritual abilities and responsibilities.

Christine was also influenced by Giovanni Boccaccio's *Concerning Famous Women* (see box in Murasaki Shikibu entry), and like Boccaccio, she examined a number of women from history. The extent to which she imitated Boccaccio's approach has been debated by critics since then, but it is clear that Christine's attitude toward her subject was quite different from that of Boccaccio. He left contemporary women out of his narrative, he said, because there were too few remarkable living women to mention.

A model for women

In 1405, Christine followed up *City of Ladies* with a companion volume entitled *The Treasure of the City of Ladies,* or *The Book of Three Virtues*. In it, she offered a model as to how women of different classes should conduct themselves in society. Her purpose was not to put anyone in their place; rather, it was to help women have dignity in a world that often tried to take it from them.

Over the years that followed, as France was embroiled in the catastrophes brought on by the Hundred Years War (1337–1453) and other forms of unrest, Christine continued to write. Her last work, in 1429, celebrated the greatest hero on either side of that war, **Joan of Arc** (see entry). In the following year, Christine died at the age of sixty-five.

Over the next century, Christine's writing would exert a strong influence on a number of less well known female writers. Then, in the 1700s, memory of her virtually disappeared, only to be resurrected again in the late nineteenth century. Since then, interest in this independent, talented woman has continued to grow.

For More Information

Books

Dahmus, Joseph Henry. *Seven Medieval Queens*. Garden City, NY: Doubleday, 1972.

Encyclopedia of World Biography, second edition. Detroit: Gale, 1998.

The Grolier Library of Women's Biographies. Danbury, CT: Grolier Educational, 1998.

Web Sites

"Christine de Pisan (ca. 1363–ca. 1431)." [Online] Available http://mala.bc.ca/~mcneil/pisan.htm (last accessed July 26, 2000).

"Christine de Pizan." *A Celebration of Women Writers*. [Online] Available http://www.cs.cmu.edu/~mmbt/women/pisan/Christine.html (last accessed July 26, 2000).

"Christine de Pisan." [Online] Available http://www.netsrq.com/~dbois/pisan.html (last accessed July 26, 2000).

Clovis

Born c. 466
Died 511

Frankish king

Americans look to George Washington as the father of their country; but Clovis, who lived more than twelve hundred years before Washington, was the father of the French nation. He was the first significant king of the Franks, a tribe that gave its name to the entire country; and even more important, he was the first notable ruler in Western Europe following the fall of the Western Roman Empire in 476. Clovis succeeded in gaining the blessing of the Christian church in Rome, which was eager to ally itself with a new leader after the fall of the empire. He also united the peoples of what is now France and surrounding areas, establishing the foundations of the medieval political order.

Gaul and the Franks

In ancient times, France was known as Gaul, an important province of the Roman Empire. But as Roman power began to fade, the western portion of the empire was overrun by various tribes that the Romans described as all related to one another—*Germanus* in Latin. These Germanic peoples were highly

"Clovis' army was near to utter destruction. He saw the danger; his heart was stirred; he was moved to tears, and he raised his eyes to heaven, saying, 'Jesus Christ, whom Clotilde declares to be the son of the living God ... I beseech the glory of thy aid.'"

Gregory of Tours, History of the Franks

Portrait: Statues of Clovis (left) and his wife Clotilde. *Reproduced by permission of the Corbis Corporation.*

uncivilized compared to the Romans, who described them as barbarians; but this did not mean that the "barbarians" were incapable of wisdom, as Clovis's career illustrates.

Clovis came from the branch of the Franks known as the Salians, who lived along the northern coast of France. Along the Rhine River, which today forms part of the boundary between France and Germany, lived another group of Franks called Ripuarians (rip-yoo-WAYR-ee-unz). In about 450, Clovis's grandfather Merovech (MAYR-uh-vesh) declared himself king of the Salians, thus establishing what came to be known as the Merovingian (mayr-uh-VIN-jee-un) dynasty.

The Merovingians sought to adopt elements of Roman civilization, which they rightly recognized as being more advanced than theirs, while retaining their distinctly Germanic culture. This was the policy of Clovis's father, Childeric (KIL-dur-ik; died c. 481), and it would be Clovis's after he took the throne at age fifteen.

The young king and warrior

Young Clovis quickly proved his abilities as a leader, uniting the Salian and Ripuarian Franks and annexing territories to build a kingdom that included much of what is now France, Belgium, Luxembourg, the Netherlands, and western Germany. He achieved this partly through warfare, but partly through skillful negotiation, which set him apart from many "barbarian" kings who preceded him. Whereas his predecessors had typically slaughtered all the inhabitants of an area, Clovis allowed them to live, which was actually in his best interests: not only did he win their good will, but his kingdom acquired new taxpayers who added to its wealth.

One of the greatest conquests of his early career was his victory over a lingering Roman stronghold in Gaul. A group of Roman citizens had gathered under the leadership of Syagrius (sy-AG-ree-us; c. 430–486), who was destined to be the last Roman governor of the region. Near the town of Soissons (swah-SAWn) in 486, twenty-year-old Clovis led his armies to victory over Syagrius, whose forces comprised mainly hired Germanic warriors rather than Romans. Later, Clovis had Syagrius executed.

Marriage to Clotilde

Five years later, in 491, Clovis defeated the Thuringians (thur-IN-jee-unz), a Germanic people who had formerly controlled a large region to the northeast of his own kingdom. Thus he added enormous lands to his growing empire. Around this time, he sent representatives to the court of the Burgundians, yet another Germanic tribe who controlled an area in southeastern France. These visitors were there not to make war, but to assess the situation among the Burgundians, and what they discovered was not good.

The Burgundian king Chilperic (KIL-pur-ik) and his wife, they learned, had been murdered by Chilperic's brother Gundobad. That meant that the princess Clotilde (kluh-TIL-duh; c. 470–545) and her sister were orphans—and that Gundobad might try to kill them as well. Furthermore, Clovis's representatives informed him, Clotilde herself was both beautiful and intelligent. Therefore Clovis negotiated with Gundobad to secure Clotilde's safe passage to his own kingdom, where he married her in 493.

Conversion to Christianity

Clotilde was a Christian, and like most Burgundians, she adhered to the mainstream form of Christianity that would later come to be known as Roman Catholicism. By contrast, many other peoples in the region had accepted Arianism, a branch of Christianity that taught that Christ was not God, but simply another one of God's creations. This viewpoint was unacceptable to the bishop of Rome (the pope), spiritual leader of the church.

Clovis refused to accept Christianity in any form, despite the urging of his wife, but continued to worship the old gods of his people. Meanwhile Clotilde gave birth to their son, and he allowed her to have the baby baptized, or sprinkled with water as a symbol of Jesus Christ's death and rebirth. But when the boy died, Clovis took this as a bad sign from the gods. They had another son, Chlodomir (KLOH-doh-mur), and again Clotilde arranged to have him baptized. This son, too, fell ill, and Clovis told her that he would die as well, but Chlodomir recovered.

King Arthur

As most people in the English-speaking world know, there are a great number of stories surrounding King Arthur, a legendary figure who ruled England in medieval times. It was said that as a boy, Arthur had gone by the name of Wart, and had pulled a sword from a stone that no one else could remove, thus fulfilling an ancient prophecy concerning England's future king. With his beautiful queen, Guinevere (GWIN-uh-veer), Arthur reigned from his palace at Camelot, supported by the brave Knights of the Round Table and his trusted magician Merlin. There are so many stories—all of them fictional, and many involving supernatural elements—surrounding Arthur and the others that it may come as a surprise to learn that there really was a King Arthur. At the very least, there was a military leader in the 500s in what is now Wales, in the western part of Britain, and he may have served as the basis for the Arthur legend.

In 546, the historian Gildas wrote about the Battle of Mount Badon (516), in which a general named Ambrosius Aurelianus led the Celts of Britain to victory over the invading Anglo-Saxons. A number of medieval writers associated Ambrosius with Arthur, though many modern scholars dispute the claim. The next mention of Arthur came in 796 from the historian Nennias, who remembered him as a commander of the Britons who in one day killed more than nine hundred of the enemy. Supposedly Arthur died in battle in 537.

Already by Nennias's time, Arthur had slipped from history into legend, and over the centuries that followed, writers such as Geoffrey of Monmouth (MAHN-muth; c. 1100–1154); Chrétien de Troyes (kray-TYAn duh TWAH; flourished 1170); and Sir Thomas Malory (flourished 1470) added to the stories surrounding Arthur. In modern times, figures such as German composer Richard Wagner; English poet Alfred, Lord Tennyson; American novelist Mark Twain; and many others each offered their own versions of Arthurian legends.

Soon afterward, Clovis went to war against the Alemanni (al-uh-MAHN-ee), a large group of tribes to the northeast. In 496, Clovis's forces engaged the Alemanni at Tolbiacum (tawl-BY-uh-kum), near the present-day city of Cologne, Germany. According to Gregory of Tours (TOOR; 538–594), the Franks' leading historian, Clovis was losing the battle until finally in desperation he prayed to Clotilde's God for victory, promising to convert to Christianity if he won the battle. Soon afterward, the Alemanni began to flee from the Franks. True to his promise, Clovis and some three thousand

Lancelot leaving Queen Guinevere's room. One of the legendary King Arthur's Knights of the Round Table, Lancelot is said in some tales of King Arthur's court to have had a love affair with the queen. *Reproduced by permission of the Corbis Corporation.*

Stories about Arthur have formed the basis for countless poems, books, paintings, plays, operas, musicals, films, and Web sites; and yet, buried beneath all the legend, there is enough fact surrounding Arthur that he is listed in *Merriam-Webster's Biographical Dictionary* as a real human being. It is even possible that there was a Welsh princess named Guinevere, though she probably did not live in the same century as Arthur. Furthermore, the identification of Arthur with England and knighthood is historically inaccurate. Knighthood did not develop until many, many centuries after Arthur's time; and the name "England" (along with the language of English) has its roots not with Arthur's Celts or Britons but with their enemies, the invading Anglo-Saxons.

of his warriors were baptized as an outward symbol of their conversion to Christianity.

The foundations of medieval Europe

In his acceptance of mainstream Christianity rather than Arianism or some other offshoot, Clovis ensured the blessing of the pope. The latter encouraged the peoples of Clovis's kingdom, most of whom were conquered Romans and

The Arc de Triomphe in Paris, France. By designating Paris as his burial site, Clovis established the city's importance, foretelling its position as the center of the French world. *Reproduced by permission of the Corbis Corporation.*

not Franks, to support Clovis. This in turn helped bring Clovis success in campaigns against other tribes, including the Visigoths in 507, and provided the foundations for the relationship between church and government during the Middle Ages.

Clovis put in place another important foundation when he authorized the creation of a legal code, or set of laws, known as the Salic Law. Modeled on Rome's highly developed legal system, Clovis's code would govern the Franks for centuries to come. When Clovis died in 511 at the age of fifty-five, his death inaugurated another important tradition: by arranging before he died to be buried in Paris, then a small town dating back to Roman times, he established the importance of that city, which is today the undisputed center of the French world.

In generations to come, the most popular name among French kings was Louis (LOO-ee), a form of "Clovis" and thus a tribute to the fifth-century king who virtually established the nation of France. The Merovingian kingdom, however, barely outlasted Clovis. In accordance with Germanic tradition, he had divided his realms between Chlodomir and his other three sons, which greatly weakened the power of his government. Still, Clovis had set in place the idea of a unified kingdom, and some 250 years later, this concept would gain new meaning under the leadership of **Charlemagne** (see entry).

For More Information

Books

Andronik, Catherine M. *Quest for a King: Searching for the Real King Arthur.* New York: Atheneum, 1989.

Asimov, Isaac. *The Dark Ages.* Boston: Houghton Mifflin, 1968.

Crossley-Holland, Kevin. *The World of King Arthur and His Court: People, Places, Legend, and Lore.* New York: Dutton Children's Books, 1999.

Motion Pictures

Camelot. Warner Home Video, 1967.

Excalibur. Warner Home Video, 1981.

The Sword in the Stone. Walt Disney Home Video, 1963.

Web Sites

Arthur's Ring. [Online] Available http://www.geocities.com/~gkingdom/saxonshore/ringmembers.html (last accessed July 26, 2000).

"The Franks." [Online] Available http://www.btinternet.com/~mark.furnival/franks.htm (last accessed July 26, 2000).

Imperium. [Online] Available http://www.ghgcorp.com/shetler/oldimp/ (last accessed July 26, 2000).

St. Cyril

Born c. 827
Died 869

Byzantine missionary

St. Methodius

Born c. 825
Died 885

Byzantine missionary

I n 863, the brothers Cyril and Methodius went as Christian missionaries to Central Europe. There they found a people ignorant not only of the Christian message, but even of reading and writing. Before they could teach them about Jesus Christ, the two Greek missionaries had to help them develop a written language, and thus was born the Cyrillic alphabet, used today in Russia and other countries. Perhaps even more important, however, was the indirect role played by Cyril and Methodius in spreading Greek Orthodoxy to other lands—most notably Russia.

Constantine and his brother

Although Methodius (mi-THOH-dee-us) was the older of the two brothers, Cyril (SEER-ul) became more famous. Much more is known about Cyril than about his older brother—including the fact that during most of his lifetime, Cyril went by the name of Constantine.

The two boys were born in the city of Thessalonica (thes-uh-luh-NYK-uh), today called Salonika, in Greece. Their

"What was at stake was a great prize, the nature of the future Slav civilization. Two great names dominate the beginning of its shaping, those of the brothers St. Cyril and St. Methodius, priests still held in honour in the Orthodox communion."

J. M. Roberts, The Age of Diverging Traditions

St. Cyril (left) and St. Methodius. *Photograph by Gianni Dagli Orti. Reproduced by permission of the Corbis Corporation.*

hometown was then the second most important city in the Byzantine Empire, the most important being the capital at Constantinople (now Istanbul, Turkey). It was to Constantinople that fourteen-year-old Constantine went in 841, after their father died. In the capital city, the imperial chancellor Theoctistus took Constantine under his wing, and arranged for the gifted young man to study at the imperial court academy.

At the academy, Constantine studied under Photius, one of the most learned men of his time, who was destined to become patriarch of Constantinople. (The patriarch is the leading figure in Greek Orthodox Christianity, much as the pope is for Roman Catholicism.) When Constantine finished his studies, Theoctistus offered him marriage to his daughter, and a powerful position at the court; but Constantine had already made up his mind to follow spiritual pursuits. In 850, he became a professor of philosophy at the imperial academy.

The early activities of Methodius are much less well known. He was living in a monastery in northwestern Asia Minor (now Turkey) in 855, when Constantine joined him, and the two went on living there for eight years. He may also have served as governor in the province where they were born, but other than that, his early life is a mystery.

Apostles to the Slavs

Constantine, or Cyril, and Methodius would become known as "Apostles to the Slavs." An apostle is a figure in the Christian church who is sent out to teach and train others, and the Slavs were a group who populated much of Eastern Europe. In 862, Rostislav, king of Great Moravia (now part of the Czech Republic), asked the Byzantine emperor Michael III for a group of missionaries—people who travel to other lands with the aim of converting others to their religion—to come and teach the Slavic Moravians about Christianity. In particular, he asked for Constantine and Methodius, who had become famous for their abilities as scholars.

Rostislav's request had political as well as religious purposes. To his west were Germans who had embraced Roman Catholicism, and had converted the Moravians to Christianity. The fact that the Moravians looked to German priests for

Olga and Vladimir

The Greek Orthodox Church has a set of saints entirely different from those of Roman Catholicism, and among these Orthodox saints are Cyril and Methodius. Two others are Olga (879–969) and Vladimir I (V'LAHD-i-meer; c. 956–1015), both rulers of Russia who were instrumental in bringing Christianity to that country.

Before she embraced Christianity, Olga was an extremely cruel woman who punished the men who murdered her husband, Prince Igor of Kiev, by having them scalded to death. She was baptized in Constantinople in 957, and arranged for missionaries to be sent to Russia; but the Christian faith did not take hold at that time. Thus Vladimir, her grandson, grew up in a world still dominated by the old pagan gods that the Russian people of Kiev had inherited from their Viking ancestors.

In rising to a position of leadership, Vladimir had to do battle with several of his brothers (he had eleven), as well as with rival nations surrounding Kiev. He turned to Christianity not necessarily because he believed in the teachings of Jesus Christ, but because he saw political advantages in embracing the Christian faith. Becoming Christian would give Russia close political ties with the Byzantine Empire, and Vladimir liked the Christian idea of a single, all-powerful God who should never be

Vladimir I. *Reproduced by permission of the Corbis Corporation.*

questioned—just the way he expected his people to view him.

In the summer of 990, Vladimir commanded the destruction of all pagan idols in Russia, and ordered his people to undergo mass baptisms. He put in place a religious schooling system, and initiated a program of tithes, meaning that the people had to give a certain portion of their money to the church. This became unpopular, and led to a revolt by his son Yaroslav (yuh-ruh-SLAHF). Despite this uprising, which Vladimir was not able to suppress before his death, he had permanently converted Russia to Christianity.

leadership gave the Germans cultural dominance over his people, a dominance Rostislav was determined to break.

The Byzantines in turn saw political advantages to fulfilling Rostislav's request, since it would give them a chance to expand their version of Christianity deep into Europe. For many centuries, two principle branches of the Christian faith—one centered around Rome, the other on Constantinople—had been moving further and further apart. Although at that time the Greek Orthodox Church and Roman Catholic Church were still united (they would only officially split in 1054), the Byzantine and Orthodox leadership saw an opportunity to establish a strong Central European foothold, and they took it.

The Cyrillic alphabet

Arriving in Moravia, the two brothers set about their first task, which was to develop a written version of the Moravians' Slavonic language. To do this, they needed an alphabet, so they used the letters of the Greek alphabet as a foundation. This would only take them so far, however, because Slavonic had sounds unknown to the Greeks. Therefore Constantine created special symbols to reflect these.

The resulting alphabet is today known as Cyrillic, and is used in Russia, Bulgaria, Serbia, and other parts of Eastern Europe. Constantine and Methodius made it the basis for a now-dead language called Old Slavonic or Church Slavonic. During the next four years, the brothers busied themselves translating the Greek Orthodox liturgy (that is, the prewritten rites for church services, baptisms, etc.) into Slavonic. Thanks to Constantine and Methodius, the Moravians were able to build a self-sufficient church.

Rome and the end

In the autumn of 867, their mission apparently finished, the two brothers made their way toward Constantinople, bringing with them a group of men who were candidates for the Orthodox priesthood. But as they were leaving, they received an invitation from Pope Nicholas I to visit him in Rome.

Therefore they decided to go there, intending to stay just a short time before returning to Constantinople; but in fact the trip took two years, and Cyril would never see Greece again.

Pope Nicholas died while they were on their way to Rome, and the new pope, Adrian II, welcomed them in his place. Seeing an opportunity to exert his own influence in Central Europe, Adrian agreed to ordain, or formally appoint, the prospective priests the brothers brought with them.

Soon afterward, Constantine and Methodius learned that Michael III had been assassinated. This left them uncertain as to how they should proceed, since they might very well return to Constantinople and find themselves in trouble with the new emperor. Constantine, at least, did not have to make a decision: he became ill and, soon after becoming a monk and taking the new name Cyril, he died on February 14, 869. Methodius chose to go back to Moravia, where he continued to work until his own death on April 6, 885.

As it turned out, Moravia would later come under the influence of the Roman Catholic Church, and thus of Western European culture. Today the Czechs are predominantly Catholic, and use a Roman alphabet similar to that of English. The Orthodox believers driven out of Moravia spread eastward, to Bulgaria and later Russia—lands where Orthodoxy established a strong and lasting hold—in the late 800s and early 900s.

For More Information

Books

De Grunwald, Constantine. *Saints of Russia*. New York: Macmillan, 1960.

Dvornik, Francis. *The Slavs: Their Early History and Civilization*. Boston: American Academy of Arts and Sciences, 1956.

Roberts, J. M. *The Illustrated History of the World*, Volume 4: *The Age of Diverging Traditions*. New York: Oxford, 1998.

Sevastiades, Philemon D. *I Am Eastern Orthodox*. New York: PowerKids Press, 1996.

Web Sites

"Medieval Russia—Religion." [Online] Available http://www.sit.wisc.edu/~jdmiller2/knowledge/religion.html (last accessed July 26, 2000).

"Orthodox WorldLinks." *Theologic Systems.* [Online] Available http://theologic.com/links/ (last accessed July 26, 2000).

"Russian Orthodox Church (Historical Background)." [Online] Available http://www.russian-orthodox-church.org.ru/hist_en.htm (last accessed July 26, 2000).

Dante Alighieri

Born 1265
Died 1321

Italian poet

When listing the world's greatest writers, critics almost always include Dante Alighieri, whose reputation is so great that he is often identified simply as "Dante." His reputation rests primarily, but not solely, on the *Divine Comedy,* an extended poetic work depicting a journey through Hell, Purgatory, and Heaven.

A book rich in images and details, the *Divine Comedy* can be read on a number of levels. To a student of the Middle Ages, it provides a vast and varied view of the time, particularly its leading figures and its attitudes. As a work written in Italian at a time when all "serious" literature was in Latin, it formed the foundation of Italy's literature and its national consciousness.

Pivotal early events

Born in the northern Italian city of Florence, Dante Alighieri (DAHN-tay al-eeg-YEER-ee) had the first significant experience of his life when he was eight years old. It was then, in 1274, that he first met Beatrice Portinari, who was a

"Midway upon the journey of our life / I found myself within a forest dark, / For the straightforward pathway had been lost."

Divine Comedy, *opening verse*

Portrait: *Reproduced by permission of the Corbis Corporation.*

few months younger than he. Nine years later, on the threshold of adulthood, he again saw her, and instantly regarded her as a symbol of God's perfection in human form. From then until the day he died, he would love her deeply, though they never had a relationship of any kind; rather, Beatrice was Dante's muse, or the inspiration for his work.

During the course of his teens, Dante showed an early ability as a writer, and he studied under several great Florentine masters of literature. Among these was Brunetto Latini, celebrated for writing in Italian rather than Latin. Latini introduced the eighteen-year-old Dante to Guido Cavalcanti, another poet who had a great influence on the young man.

Also at eighteen, Dante inherited a modest family fortune, both of his parents having died when he was younger. Two years later, he married Gemma Donati in a union apparently arranged by their fathers years before. The couple would later have three children, and their son Pietro would grow up to become a well-known commentator on the *Divine Comedy*.

Marriage did not stop Dante from loving Beatrice, however; nor did her death in 1290, when Dante was twenty-five. It was then that he began writing poetry in earnest, attempting to overcome his grief. In the process, he also overcame the influence of his early teachers and forged his own style.

Political involvements and exile

Dante studied at a number of great universities in Western Europe, and his reaction to the death of Beatrice brought on an intensive reading of ancient and early medieval philosophers. In 1289, however, he left school to enlist in the Florentine army, and fought in the Battle of Campaldino that year.

Italy at that time was torn by a church-state conflict that pitted the Guelphs (GWELFZ), supporters of the Roman Catholic Church, against the Ghibellines (GIB-uh-leenz), who backed the Holy Roman emperor. In Florence, the political division was even more complicated due to a split between the Black Guelphs and the White Guelphs. Dante sided with the White Guelphs, who took a less hard-line approach toward the Ghibellines than the Black Guelphs did; but the pope, leader of the Catholic Church, put his support behind the Black Guelphs.

In the years between 1295 and 1301, Dante became intensely involved in politics and held a number of public offices. The Blacks staged a coup (KOO), or sudden takeover, in Florence in 1301, and forced all Whites to leave the city. Among those banished was Dante, who was stripped of all his possessions and forbidden from re-entering the city the following year. He would spend the remainder of his life wandering throughout Italy, living in a variety of cities.

This painting by Eugène Delacroix (de-la-KWAH; 1798–1863) shows the Roman poet Virgil leading Dante through Hell and Purgatory in Dante's *Divine Comedy*. *Reproduced by permission of the Corbis Corporation.*

Dante's other writings

Dante had written his first major work in 1293, during the five-year period between Beatrice's death and the beginnings of his political involvement. This work was *La vita nuova*, or *The New Life*, a collection of poems to Beatrice, which critics praised for its "sweet new style" and its refreshing approach to love as a spiritual experience.

Omar Khayyám

Like Dante, Omar Khayyám (c. 1048–c. 1131) was a poet, but Khayyám established an equally great reputation as a philosopher, mathematician, and astronomer. Khayyám, who lived in Persia (now Iran), wrote a paper on algebra that is considered one of the most significant works on that subject from medieval times.

He is most famous to Western readers, however, from the *Rubáiyát,* a collection of verses first translated into English in 1859 by the English poet and scholar Edward FitzGerald. Among the most famous lines from the *Rubáiyát* as translated by FitzGerald is "A Book of Verses underneath the Bough, / A Jug of Wine, a loaf of bread— and Thou / Beside me singing in the Wilder-ness— / Oh, Wilderness were Paradise enow!" The last word is a poetic version of *enough,* and the line means, in effect, "with you even a wilderness is paradise."

Little is known about Khayyám's life, except that he was commissioned by Malik Shah, sultan of the Seljuk Turks, to work on reforming the calendar. He also helped plan an observatory in Persia, and spent his later years teaching mathematics and astrology. Seven centuries after his death, the rediscovery of his work by FitzGerald brought on an explosion of interest in Khayyám, who became perhaps more famous in the modern West than he had been in the medieval Middle East.

In exile, he wrote another collection of poetry, *Il convivio* (*The Banquet*; 1304–7); and two significant prose works. The first of these was *De vulgari eloquentia* (*Eloquence in the Vernacular Tongue*; 1303–7), a defense of Italian literature. Ironically, *De vulgari* was in Latin, as was *De monarchia* (*On Monarchy*; c. 1313), an examination of Dante's political views. By far the greatest of his works, however, was the *Divine Comedy,* which he began in 1308 and completed just before his death thirteen years later.

The *Divine Comedy*

The term "divine" is a reference to God, an abiding presence throughout the narrative. As for the "comedy" part, it is not a comedy in the traditional sense; rather, the term refers to the fact that the story, told in a series of 100 "chapters" called cantos, has a happy ending. Dante placed the events of the *Divine Comedy* at Easter Weekend 1300, when he was—as he wrote in the opening lines of Canto I—"Midway upon the journey of our life" (thirty-five years old).

The *Divine Comedy* depicts Dante's journey into the depths of the Inferno or Hell, guided by the departed soul of the Roman poet Virgil (70–19 B.C.). At the end of the *Inferno,* he is forced to leave Virgil behind as he travels into Purgatory, a place of punishment for people working out their salvation and earning their way into Heaven or Paradise. In these two sections, his guide is Beatrice.

The *Divine Comedy* is not meant to be understood as a literal story; rather, it is an allegory or symbolic tale. It concerns such spiritual matters as faith, revelation, and eternity; it also addresses the political issues of Dante's time. Clearly, however, there is something eternal and universal in the *Divine Comedy,* and this helps to explain the continued appreciation for this work.

In 1373, more than half a century after Dante died, Florence—the city that had once rejected him—honored his memory by commissioning Petrarch (PEE-trark; 1304–1374) to deliver a series of lectures on the *Divine Comedy.* Since that time, Dante has been in and out of favor, depending on the attitudes of the era; but overall his reputation continues to grow with the passage of time.

This fifteenth-century illustration from the manuscript of Dante's *Divine Comedy* shows Virgil and Dante with the Condemned Souls in Eternal Ice.
Reproduced by permission of the Corbis Corporation.

For More Information

Books

Dante Alighieri. *The Divine Comedy of Dante Alighieri.* Translated by Henry Wadsworth Longfellow. Boston: Houghton, Mifflin and Company, 1906.

Halliwell, Sarah, editor. *The Renaissance: Artists and Writers*. Austin, TX: Raintree Steck-Vaughn, 1998.

Holmes, George. *Dante*. New York: Farrar, Straus, 1980.

Web Sites

Dante Alighieri on the Web. [Online] Available http://www.geocities.com/Athens/9039/main.htm (last accessed July 26, 2000).

Digital Dante. [Online] Available http://www.ilt.columbia.edu/projects/dante/ (last accessed July 26, 2000).

"Omar Khayyam." [Online] Available http://www-groups.dcs.st-and.ac.uk/~history/Mathematicians/Khayyam.html (last accessed July 26, 2000).

Rubaiyat of Omar Khayyam. [Online] Available http://www.promotional-guide.com/ok/ (last accessed July 26, 2000).

The World of Dante. [Online] Available http://www.iath.virginia.edu/dante/ (last accessed July 26, 2000).

Zahoor, Dr. A. "Omar Al-Khayyam, 1044–1123 C.E." [Online] Available http://users.erols.com/zenithco/khayyam.html (last accessed July 26, 2000).

El Cid

Born c. 1043
Died 1099

Spanish warrior and hero

The pages of medieval history are filled with figures whose biographies are equal parts legend and fact—or in some cases, more legend than fact—from the saintly **Rabia al-Adawiyya** (see entry) to the devilish Vlad Tepes (see box in Tamerlane entry). Perhaps nowhere is this mixture of fact and fiction more evident than in the life of Rodrigo Díaz de Vivar, better known as El Cid.

Mythologized as a valiant Christian knight who fought heroically against the Muslims, he was in reality a soldier of fortune who spent most of his career in conflict with a Christian king, and who at one time served a Muslim emir. At least parts of the legend are accurate: El Cid was without question a brave and talented warrior, and he was at least as honorable as most knights of his time. Certainly there is an air of romance even to the tale of the *real* El Cid, and it is on this foundation of air that the legend was built.

Trained as a warrior

In about 1043, Rodrigo Díaz de Vivar (rohth-REE-goh

Portrait.

Harun al-Rashid

Harun al-Rashid (hah-ROON; rah-SHEED; 766–809) served as caliph or ruler over the Arab Muslim empire at the height of its glory under the Abbasid (uh-BAHS-id) dynasty. Like El Cid, he also became a figure of legend, thanks to his association with the famous *Thousand and One Nights,* known in the West as *The Arabian Nights.*

The name Harun al-Rashid—sometimes rendered as *Haroun* and/or *ar-Rashid*—is Arabic for "Aaron the Upright." Born in what is now Iran, he was the third son of the caliph al-Mahdi and his wife al-Khayzuran (kay-zoo-RAHN), a former slave who became the most influential woman in the caliphate. She used her sway to help Harun rise to power following the death of his father, and at the young age of twenty, he assumed control over the most powerful empire in the world at that time.

During the late 770s and early 780s, before he became caliph, Harun was engaged in military conflicts against the Byzantine Empire, the second most powerful force in the region. His leadership of the troops was largely symbolic, however: the real control rested with Ibn Khalid (IB'n kah-LEED), his advisor. Ibn Khalid and his two sons would hold key positions in Harun's court.

Harun spent much of his reign in conflict with the Byzantines. With **Irene of Athens** (see entry), he established a successful relationship of non-aggression (neither side would attack the other), but his relations with her successors were not as good. Wisely preferring to use peaceful means to protect the caliphate wherever possible, Harun established a special military province to act as a buffer on the Byzantine frontier.

The threats were not just outside the caliphate: within its borders, Harun had to deal with revolts by a number of nation-

dee-AHZ duh BEE-bahdr) was born to a noble family in the Spanish kingdom of Castile (kas-TEEL). By that time, Muslim forces had ruled southern Spain for three centuries, while Christian kingdoms dominated the north. Of these kingdoms, Castile—so named for its many castles—was the most powerful, and Rodrigo's family belonged to its highly esteemed warrior class. He was well connected on both his mother's and father's sides, and as a child learned to read and write—unusual skills in medieval times, even among the nobility.

His father died when he was fifteen years old, and Rodrigo went to live in the household of Fernando I, king of Castile. Fernando's son, Prince Sancho, took Rodrigo under his

Harun al-Rashid. *Reproduced by permission of the Hulton-Getty Picture Library.*

as their father, and after his death their greed for power led them into war with one another.

The era of Harun is remembered as a golden age, one closely associated with the *Thousand and One Nights.* The sultan in the latter book, whose young bride tells him a new tale every night, is said to have been modeled in part on Harun. Also famous is an exchange between Harun and **Charlemagne** (see entry), to whom Harun reportedly sent the gift of an elephant. It is perhaps a measure of Harun's prestige, and that of the Abbasid caliphate, that nowhere in the Abbasids' official histories is his contact with Charlemagne—the most important figure in the history of Western Europe during the early medieval period—even mentioned.

al groups seeking independence from their masters in Baghdad, the Abbasid capital. Toward the end of his life, he sought to ensure a smooth succession through his sons, but they proved not to be as cool-headed

wing, teaching him military arts that would serve him well in times to come. Though the kingdoms of the north were by then engaged in the Reconquista (ray-kawn-KEES-tah), an effort to place Muslim lands under Christian rule, Rodrigo's first taste of battle at age twenty came in a conflict between two Christian kingdoms, Castile and Aragon (AHdR-uh-gawn).

Conflict between brothers

In 1065, when Rodrigo was twenty-two years old, Fernando died. As eldest son, Sancho received Castile, while his younger brothers Alfonso and García respectively inherited the smaller kingdoms of León (lay-OHN) and Galicia (gah-LEETH-ee-ah). This situation was a recipe for future conflict, but in the meantime, Rodrigo was given the important position of royal standard bearer, which put him in direct control over the king's bodyguard.

Rodrigo proved a faithful servant to his lord, and distinguished himself in battle numerous times. In 1067, he led forces against Sancho's rivals in the kingdoms of Aragon and Navarre (nuh-VAHdR). Soon Sancho and his brother Alfonso squared off against one another, and forces led by Rodrigo scored a decisive victory over Alfonso at Golpejera (gohl-pay-HAY-dah) in 1072. Shortly afterward, Sancho became king of León as well as Castile, and he banished Alfonso.

Alfonso triumphant

Sancho held his new position for less than a year: in the fall of 1072, he was assassinated, and suddenly Alfonso assumed control of Castile and León. Not surprisingly, Rodrigo was not among Alfonso's favorites, yet the new king made no move to attack his old enemy. Instead, Rodrigo was stripped of all rank, and military positions were given to various leaders from León, include Count García Ordóñez (ohdr-DOHN-yez).

In 1074, however, Rodrigo recovered much of his former prestige by marrying Jimena Díaz (hee-MAY-nah), the king's niece. It is likely the king himself arranged the marriage, proof that Rodrigo's standing at the court had risen once again. But the soldier would not remain in his master's good graces for long.

Fall from grace

In 1079, Rodrigo made a fatal blunder from the standpoint of his reputation with Alfonso. He attacked a group of mercenaries, or men who fight for pay, in the service of Granada. Though Granada's rulers were Muslims, the men in the party seized and imprisoned by Rodrigo were from León—and they included Ordóñez, one of Alfonso's favorites. Instead of letting them go when he realized they were well connected, however, Rodrigo pressed Ordóñez's family for ransom money, an act that infuriated the king.

Two years later, in the summer of 1081, Moorish bandits from Toledo (doh-LAY-doh) attacked a Castilian stronghold. The king was away, and Rodrigo led the defending force, which chased the invaders to Toledo and proceeded to take some 7,000 prisoners. Instead of being overjoyed when he learned of this, Alfonso was angered that Rodrigo had acted without his authorization, and he ordered the soldier banished from Castile.

Years as a mercenary

Rodrigo spent the next five years in Zaragoza (zah-duh-GOH-zah), serving the Muslim ruler al-Mu'tamin (mü-tah-MEEN). In 1082, he led al-Mu'tamin's troops to a major victory over Count Ramón Berenguer II (bayr-un-GAYR) of Barcelona. There followed a series of successes, and even after al-Mu'tamin died in 1085, Rodrigo remained loyal to his successor.

In May 1085, Alfonso seized Toledo, which had been in Muslim hands for three centuries, and laid siege to Zaragoza. This prompted the Muslims to call in help from the Almoravids (al-muh-RAH-vedz), who controlled Morocco. The Almoravids, who soon became the dominant Islamic force in Spain, defeated Alfonso in battle on October 23, 1086, and this prompted him to open up communication with Rodrigo once again.

Attempts at reconciliation with Alfonso

Alfonso soon reinstated Rodrigo, and placed him in charge of an army. In 1089, however, Rodrigo failed to reinforce Alfonso's troops in an attack against the Almoravids, and this infuriated the king. Rodrigo's wife and children were briefly imprisoned, and Rodrigo himself was exiled for good.

He moved to Spain's eastern coast, where he became a warlord who answered to no king. This worried Berenguer, who raised a force against him in May 1090, but the outcome of this engagement was that Rodrigo captured Berenguer. As a result, he obtained ransom money and official recognition of his power, and by the end of the year, he held most of the region aside from the city of Valencia.

Rodrigo's interest in Valencia would thwart yet another attempted reconciliation with Alfonso. It so happened that Alfonso, who sent troops into the area in 1092, also wanted Valencia. Rodrigo retaliated by invading Castile and devastating lands under the control of his old foe Ordóñez, acts that resulted in a withdrawal of Alfonso's forces from Valencia. Rodrigo began a siege against Valencia in the summer of 1093, and the city fell to him a year later, on June 15, 1094.

The legendary El Cid

Rodrigo and other leaders of Christian Spain were not the only ones who considered Valencia important: when the Almoravids learned of the city's conquest by Rodrigo, they quickly sent a force against him. Leading a much smaller army, Rodrigo devastated the Almoravids in battle on October 14, 1094—the first time the Moorish invaders had suffered a defeat since their arrival in Spain eight years before.

Ironically, the man who had spent so much of his life in the saddle, sword in hand, died peacefully in his bed on July 10, 1099. Following his death, his wife Jimena struggled to maintain control over Valencia, a conflict in which Alfonso came to her aid. After three years, however, Alfonso could no longer defend the city, and he urged Jimena to give it up and come to Castile. Valencia fell to the Almoravids in May 1102, and it would not return to Christian hands until 1238.

By that time, Rodrigo's life story was being turned into a myth, which became the *Poema de mio Cid,* a work of anonymous authorship sometimes translated as *The Lay of the Cid*. The nickname El Cid, meaning "The Master" in Arabic, actually came from Rodrigo's enemies, who were some of his greatest admirers. Thus the Arab historian Ibn Bassam wrote that the legendary foe of his people "was one of the miracles of God." To Spaniards, El Cid became immortal as a romantic hero, a defiant individual who triumphed over powers much greater than himself.

For More Information

Books

Audisio, Gabriel. *Harun al-Rashid, Caliph of Baghdad.* New York: R. M. McBride & Company, 1931.

Clot, André. *Haroun al-Rashid and the World of the Thousand and One Nights.* Translated by John Howe. New York: New Amsterdam Book, 1989.

Goldston, Robert C. *The Legend of the Cid.* Illustrated by Stephane. Indianapolis, IN: Bobbs-Merrill, 1963.

The Lay of the Cid. Translated by R. Selden Bose and Leonard Bacon. Berkeley: University of California Press, 1919.

McCaughrean, Geraldine. *El Cid.* Illustrated by Victor G. Ambrus. New York: Oxford University Press, 1989.

Web Sites

"Abbasid Caliphate (Baghdad): 750–1258." [Online] Available http://www.campus.northpark.edu/history/WebChron/Islam/Abbasid.html (last accessed July 26, 2000).

"Battles of Rodrigo Díaz de Vivar 'El Cid.'" [Online] Available http://rococo.ele.cie.uva.es/ismael/med/cid.html (last accessed July 26, 2000).

"Harun al-Rashid." [Online] Available http://www.deepfield.com/anoot/harun_al.htm (last accessed July 26, 2000).

"Legends—Paladins and Princes—The Cid." [Online] Available http://www.legends.dm.net/paladins/cid.html (last accessed July 26, 2000).

"The Song of El Cid." [Online] Available http://kuhttp.cc.ukans.edu/kansas/medieval/108/info/el_cid.html (last accessed July 26, 2000).

Eleanor of Aquitaine

Born 1122
Died 1204

Queen of France and England

Eleanor of Aquitaine was a rare individual indeed. As wife of Louis VII, she ruled France, only to divorce her husband and marry Henry of Anjou, who would later make her queen of England. Marriage may have gotten her into positions of power, but what Eleanor did with that power was her own special gift. Both shrewd and intelligent, she was a highly cultured woman who managed to stay atop the shifting political structures of Western Europe, and at the same time cultivated learning and the arts in her lands.

The court at Aquitaine

During her long and varied life, Eleanor often found herself (or in many cases, put herself) at the center of conflicts. It was perhaps a trait she learned from her father, Duke William X of Aquitaine in France. William dared to disagree with **Bernard of Clairvaux** (klayr-VOH; see entry), a religious leader who was perhaps the most powerful man in Western Europe—even more so than the pope, official head of the Catholic Church.

"Seek, my child, those things which make for peace. Cease to stir up the king against the Church and urge him a better course of action. If you will promise to do this, I in my turn promise to entreat the merciful Lord to grant you offspring."

Bernard of Clairvaux's advice to Eleanor

Portrait: *Reproduced by permission of Archive Photos, Inc.*

Besides the tendency to quarrel, an interest in the arts seemed to run in Eleanor's family. Her grandfather, William IX, became distinguished as a troubadour (TROO-buh-dohr), a type of poet in medieval France. Eleanor herself grew up surrounded by music and literature at her father's court, a French center of culture.

A powerful fifteen-year-old

In 1137, however, fifteen-year-old Eleanor was suddenly jolted from what might have been a quiet, easy life when her father died without a male heir. As his oldest child, Eleanor became not only duchess of Aquitaine, but countess of Poitou (pwah-TÜ). Any man who married her would control even more of France than the king did, and this put Eleanor in danger of kidnapping and forced marriage.

It so happened that before his death, William had asked the king to become Eleanor's guardian. Now King Louis VI (LOO-ee) took her under his wing in a way that also served his own interests, by arranging her marriage to his son, the future King Louis VII (c. 1120–1180; ruled 1137–1180). Shortly after the wedding, Louis VI died, making Eleanor—not yet sixteen years old—queen of France.

Queen of France

Louis VII seemed more suited to a career as a monk or priest than as king of France, and in fact he had been raised for a life in the church, and would never have become king if his older brother had not died in a riding accident. Thus Louis was not inclined to make trouble for the pope and other Catholic leaders, whereas Eleanor had a mind of her own.

Eleanor's younger sister Petronille (pet-roh-NEEL) was having an affair with Count Ralph of Vermandois (vayr-mun-DWAH), and she wanted to make an honest woman of herself by marrying him. The problem was that Ralph already had a wife, and divorce was not possible under church laws. The only way around this was to have a marriage annulled, or declared illegal, so Eleanor arranged this for her sister.

As it turned out, however, Ralph's former wife had powerful friends, not least of whom was the pope, who lashed out at France with all the power he had. This put Louis VII, a reluctant participant in the conflict, in a difficult position. Finally Bernard of Clairvaux stepped in and helped settle the dispute. He also advised Eleanor that if she would quit making trouble with the church, God would give her the thing for which she had long been hoping: a child.

The Second Crusade

Eleanor did stop quarreling with the church, and in 1145 she did give birth to a daughter, Marie. Shortly afterward, Bernard organized the Second Crusade (1147–49), an effort to win control of the Holy Land for Christian forces, and Louis took part as a means of winning back the favor of the church.

Eleanor went with him, and in the Syrian city of Antioch (AN-tee-ahk), an important crusader stronghold, she met her uncle, Raymond of Toulouse (tuh-LOOS). Raymond was only twelve years older than she, and they instantly became close. The nature of their relationship has long been disputed by historians; regardless of whether they became lovers, however, they were certainly close friends.

During their long hours talking, Raymond became the first person to learn of Eleanor's misgivings regarding her marriage. "I thought I had married a king," she told him, "but I find I have married a monk." Raymond suggested that she could obtain an annulment on the basis of consanguinity (kahn-sang-GWIN-i-tee)—blood relationship, or the fact that she and Louis were too closely related.

In fact medieval monarchs and nobles often married close relatives, but it made for a good excuse, and Eleanor announced to Louis that due to consanguinity and a desire to remain in Antioch with Raymond, she was not returning to France. Louis, however, forced her to return.

Divorce and remarriage

Despite the birth of a second daughter, not to mention help from the pope in sorting out their marital problems,

King John

Though he came from a distinguished family—son of Henry II and Eleanor of Aquitaine, brother of Richard the Lion-Hearted—King John of England (1167–1216; ruled 1199–1216) was not a great man. Yet his very lack of greatness has benefited the world more than anything his more admirable relatives did: it was John's greediness and cruelty that caused the drafting of the Magna Carta (1215), one of the most important documents in the history of free government.

John was the youngest of Henry's sons, and in spite of the fact that from an early age he showed himself to be spiteful, childish, and domineering, he was his father's favorite. Henry had already promised most of his lands to his older sons, but he set about securing properties for John. The latter finally received dominion over Ireland, but mismanaged it so badly that he had to surrender control. In the meantime, Henry's attempts to grab land for John put him into conflict with his wife and other sons, who led a revolt against him. John himself joined in the revolt against his father, and this was a crushing blow to Henry, who died in 1189.

No sooner had Richard become king than he went away to take part in the Third Crusade (1189–92), leaving John as his heir if anything should happen to him. John lost no time in conspiring to take the throne, and when Richard heard about this, he tried to return from the crusade. On the way, he was kidnapped and taken prisoner in Austria, where he remained for two years. It is said that John actually sent letters to Richard's captors, asking them not to release him.

But the English nobility and their people, with whom Richard was very popular, raised the money for his ransom, and in 1194 Richard returned to England. Rather than deal harshly with John, however, Richard let him be. Five years later, in 1199, Richard died from an infected arrow wound, and John became undisputed king of England.

John proceeded to mismanage England as he once had Ireland, taxing the people so ferociously that many starved. Looking for a replacement, his nobles were willing to put their support behind John's

Eleanor's marriage to Louis was doomed. In 1152, she left him, and soon afterward arranged to have her marriage annulled. As a woman possessing huge lands, however, she could not afford to remain unmarried for long; therefore just two months after the end of her first marriage, she married a man eleven years her junior, Henry, count of Anjou (ahn-ZHOO; 1133–1189).

nephew Arthur, count of Anjou, but in 1204 Arthur was murdered—some say by John himself. One person who claimed that John had committed the murder was the French king Philip, who used this as an excuse to take over most English holdings in France.

Forced back to England, John imposed even more heavy taxes on the people, and began robbing them of all their possessions as a way of adding to his fortunes. He also quarreled with the Roman Catholic Church, and eventually Pope **Innocent III** (see entry) placed a ban on all church activities—including weddings—in England. For six years, no church bells rang in the entire country.

This did not bother John, who helped himself to all lands formerly controlled by the church; but when he learned that France was about to launch an invasion against him, he turned to the pope for help. As a sign of repentance, he "gave" England to the pope, who could now demand huge taxes of the English people each year. By 1214, the church taxes alone were equal to nearly one-third of the nation's yearly income, and the burden became too much for the noblemen of England.

Lacking a replacement for John, the nobles decided they would set down some new rules. This they did in 1215 with the Magna Carta, or "Great Charter," a document containing sixty-three articles concerning the rights of the nobility. The noblemen forced John to sign it at a meeting in a meadow called Runnymeade along the banks of the Thames (TEMZ) River.

John had no choice but to sign the document, yet he spent the rest of his life—just one year, as it turned out—behaving just as he had before. Now, however, the English lords had a document spelling out their rights, and the obligations of the king. This led ultimately to the creation of Parliament, the body of representatives that today holds the real power in England. Thus the Magna Carta, originally designed to protect only the upper classes, became a model for government by the people, and later influenced the U.S. Declaration of Independence and Constitution.

Henry's mother Matilda was a grandchild of **William the Conqueror** (see entry), as was the reigning English king, Stephen. Stephen had usurped, or seized, the throne from Matilda, and Henry fought with him for control. The outcome was an agreement, the Treaty of Winchester (1153), which stated that when Stephen died, Henry would take the throne. Stephen died in 1154, and thus within two years, Eleanor went from being queen of France to queen of England.

Henry's accession to the English throne established the ruling House of Plantagenet (plan-TAJ-uh-net), destined to rule for nearly 250 years; and during much of that time, England and France would find themselves at war. The roots of the problem went back to the marriage of Henry and Eleanor, which combined the French duchies of Aquitaine and Anjou, and (following Henry's accession to the English throne) placed both of those territories under the rule of England. Thus the English royal house controlled more of France than the French crown did. Perhaps Eleanor could have eased things by asking the king's permission before marrying Henry—but since the king happened to be her ex-husband, she knew he would never give his consent.

Conflict between father and sons

Eleanor bore Henry numerous children over the years from 1153 to 1166, including four sons. During much of this time, Henry was away, overseeing his lands in France, and Eleanor ruled England as regent. Then in 1168, Henry returned full control of Aquitaine—the ruler of which he had become at the time of their marriage—to Eleanor, and she moved there.

The marriage with Henry had not turned out to be much happier than the one with Louis, though for opposite reasons. Certainly Eleanor could not accuse Henry of being monk-like: he was a lusty, battle-hardened warrior, an unfaithful husband and a selfish father.

In 1170, Eleanor persuaded Henry to follow a French custom and crown his eldest son Henry while he continued to reign. The father agreed to do so, but did not permit the son—who never lived to reign, and is known to history as Henry the Young King—to hold any power.

Eleanor became increasingly displeased with Henry's unwillingness to pass on the throne to one of their children. Therefore over the course of the 1170s and the early 1180s, she joined forces with Louis VII, who apparently let bygones be bygones, especially because he and Eleanor now had a mutual enemy. Together with her sons, they periodically waged war against Henry. But the king held on to power, and in 1186 he had Eleanor imprisoned in Salisbury Castle.

Richard and John

Eleanor spent three years in prison, gaining release upon Henry's death in 1189. For such a well-traveled and cultured person, those years of confinement were especially difficult—not to mention the fact that by now she was almost seventy years old. But Eleanor still had many good years left, and she devoted them to her sons—or rather to her eldest surviving son, **Richard I** (the Lion-Hearted; see entry).

Richard took the throne upon the death of his father, and Eleanor became his trusted (and very powerful) counselor. She oversaw Richard's affairs, arranging a beneficial marriage for him and in 1192 putting down a revolt led by another son, John (see box). When Richard was kidnapped following the Third Crusade, she ran the country, and it was she who delivered his ransom to Germany in the dead of winter, 1194. Therefore she was all the more devastated when Richard, having returned to England, died from an infected arrow wound in 1199.

John kneels down before King Richard I, asking forgiveness for his attempt to take the throne from Richard. *Reproduced by permission of the Corbis Corporation.*

This left John, who was as greedy and cruel as Richard was noble, on the throne. Though John was not Eleanor's first choice for king, he was all that she had left, and she supported him when Arthur of Anjou, one of her grandsons, tried to claim the throne. Despite her help, John proved a failure as a king, and lost most of the family's French possessions.

At least Aquitaine remained in Eleanor's control, and as her life drew to a close, she possessed little more than she had when it began. Still suffering from the loss of Richard, she went to live with the nuns at the abbey of Fontevrault (fawn-tuh-VROH), where her favorite son, Richard, and her second husband were buried. She died in the spring of 1204, at the age of eighty-two.

For More Information

Books

Asimov, Isaac. *The Shaping of England.* Boston: Houghton Mifflin, 1969.

Ayars, James Sterling. *We Hold These Truths: From Magna Carta to the Bill of Rights.* New York: Viking Press, 1977.

Brooks, Polly Schoyer. *Queen Eleanor, Independent Spirit of the Medieval World: A Biography of Eleanor of Aquitaine.* New York: J. B. Lippincott, 1983.

Davis, Mary Lee. *Women Who Changed History: Five Famous Queens of Europe.* Minneapolis: Lerner Publications, 1975.

Kaplan, Zoë Coralnik. *Eleanor of Aquitaine.* Introduction by Arthur M. Schlesinger Jr. New York: Chelsea House Publishers, 1987.

Motion Pictures

The Lion in Winter. Columbia Tristar Home Video, 1968.

Web Sites

"Eleanor of Aquitaine, Queen of England." [Online] Available http://www.geocities.com/Athens/Aegean/7545/Eleanor.html (last accessed July 26, 2000).

"Female Hero: Eleanor of Aquitaine." *Women in World History.* [Online] Available http://www.womeninworldhistory.com/heroine2.html (last accessed July 26, 2000).

"Magna Carta." *National Archives and Records Administration.* [Online] Available http://www.nara.gov/exhall/charters/magnacarta/mag-main.html (last accessed July 26, 2000).

English Scholars, Thinkers, and Writers

Alcuin
Born c. 735
Died 804

English scholar and teacher

St. Anselm of Canterbury
Born c. 1033
Died 1109

Italian-English church leader and philosopher

Thomas à Becket
Born 1118
Died 1170

English church leader and chancellor

William of Ockham
Born c. 1290
Died 1349

English philosopher

Geoffrey Chaucer
Born c. 1340
Died 1400

English author and poet

Because it is an island and geographically separated from the European continent, England's civilization became quite different from the rest of Europe. Successive waves of invasion gave it many influences, contributing to the broad reach of the English language. Likewise England developed an emphasis on freedom and individualism unmatched among European nations. These concepts became central to the foundation of America, and thus all Americans—regardless of ethnic heritage—can claim ties to the English traditions.

The five men profiled below, all noted as scholars, thinkers, and/or writers, each contributed to the development of the English mind. Each man deserves far more attention than space permits, because each in his own way changed the world.

Alcuin

A scholar trained in the church, Alcuin (AL-kwin) is best known for his work as headmaster over a school in France, a job he was given by **Charlemagne** (see entry) in

> "Defend me with your sword, and I will support you with my pen."
>
> *Promise allegedly made to Emperor Ludwig IV by William of Ockham*

782. By that time he was almost fifty years old, and had long directed a cathedral school in England, but on returning from a trip to Rome, he met the emperor. It was a time known to some historians as the Dark Ages, when learning had nearly come to a standstill: few people could read and write, and even those literate few had a poor command over Latin, the language of the educated. Thus Charlemagne was badly in need of a scholar to teach the nobility and priests of his empire, as well as the royal family.

Under Alcuin's direction, the palace school at Charlemagne's capital trained a new generation of administrators in a manner that resembled that of the ancient Romans. This contributed significantly to the "Carolingian renaissance," a bright spot of renewed interest in learning during the dark centuries from 500 to 1000. Also notable was Alcuin's reorganization of the liturgy—that is, the procedural instructions for church services—in Charlemagne's empire. This would have an enormous impact far beyond Alcuin's lifetime: many of the reforms he established remain in use among French Catholics to this day.

So, too, would his training of the new educated class in France, Germany, and other lands ruled by Charlemagne. In the latter part of Alcuin's life, just after his retirement in 796, Viking attacks on the British Isles threatened to extinguish the lamp of learning: for instance, the library at York, one of the most important in England, was completely destroyed by the invaders. It was only through the efforts of men from the European continent—students of Alcuin's students—that the scholarly tradition was reestablished in England.

St. Anselm of Canterbury

Though born in Italy, Anselm is best remembered for his work in England. He first visited in 1078, when he was about forty-five and serving as an abbot, or head of a monastery, in France. Nine years later, a dying **William the Conqueror** (see entry) sent for Anselm to read him his last rites, but the abbot arrived too late.

At that time the Archbishop of Canterbury, leading priest among English Christians, was a former teacher of Anselm's named Lanfranc. Lanfranc died in May 1089, and

William's son William II (sometimes known as William Rufus) was so determined to control the English church that he refused to appoint a new archbishop for four years. After he almost died in 1093, however, William became fearful that he was disobeying God by not appointing a new archbishop, and would be punished for doing so. He chose Anselm for the role.

The result was a series of conflicts between Anselm and William that would persist throughout the latter's reign. For instance, the king tried to stop Anselm from traveling to Rome in 1095 to receive a pallium, a woolen shoulder covering that symbolized papal approval, from Urban II (see box in Innocent III entry). Despite William's attempts to limit his influence, Anselm did his best to help the king, and personally blessed William before leaving on a second trip to Rome in late 1097. While he was away, Anselm completed his most important work, *Why God Became Man;* and William, who had tried to seize all of Anselm's property, died.

St. Anselm of Canterbury. *Reproduced by permission of the Library of Congress.*

Initially Anselm's relationship with William's brother Henry I was no better than it had been with William, but the two finally reached an agreement in Normandy in July 1105. Soon afterward, at the Conference of Westminster, church and state spelled out their mutual obligations in a written agreement. The latter became the model for the Concordat of Worms (1122), which settled a similar dispute between the pope and the Holy Roman emperor. Anselm died in Canterbury on April 21, 1109, and in 1163 a new archbishop of Canterbury put him forward for canonization, or sainthood.

Thomas à Becket

That archbishop was Thomas à Becket (the *à* is pronounced "uh"; often he is simply called Thomas Becket). A

Thomas à Becket. *Reproduced by permission of the Granger Collection Ltd.*

member of a distinguished family, Thomas grew up to lead a life of privilege that included an education at Paris, then Europe's leading center of learning. His fortunes changed, however, when he was twenty-one: his mother's death and his father's subsequent financial problems forced his return to England.

Young Thomas soon became personal secretary to Theobald, archbishop of Canterbury, and this job gave him considerable opportunities for travel. In 1154, when Thomas was thirty-six, a new royal house took control of England under the leadership of Henry II, husband of **Eleanor of Aquitaine** and father of **Richard I** (see entries) and the future King John (see box in Eleanor of Aquitaine entry). Theobald recommended Thomas to Henry, who appointed him as his chancellor—one of the king's key advisors—in 1155.

For the next six years, Thomas enjoyed the power and privilege that went with a position at the king's right hand. Yet when Theobald died in 1161, events took a quite different turn. Henry appointed Thomas to the archbishop's seat in 1162, and probably assumed that his former chancellor would remain his faithful servant. Thomas, however, took the role of archbishop seriously, seeing himself as a representative of God rather than as a lackey to a king. This conviction would bring about his undoing.

The first major dispute between king and archbishop involved the legal rights of church officials who committed crimes under the secular (non-church) laws of the land. Henry maintained that they should be tried in government courts, whereas Thomas held that their trials should take place in church courts. This conflict became so heated that in 1164, Thomas fled England to seek refuge with Eleanor's former husband, Louis VII of France.

During his six years of exile, Thomas carried on lengthy negotiations with Henry, who in 1170 arranged for the coronation of his son, known to history as Henry the Young King. Infuriated that Henry would take it upon himself to crown a new king—a privilege that belonged exclusively to the archbishop—Thomas returned to Canterbury. Equally angered, Henry was at dinner one night when he demanded of his guests, "Who will rid me of the turbulent priest?"

Four knights responded, and hastened to Canterbury, where on December 29, 1170, they murdered Thomas while he was praying. As a result, Thomas became a widely admired martyr, canonized just three years after his death. The act of assassination had an effect exactly opposite of that which Henry had desired.

William of Ockham

Like the three men profiled above, William of Ockham (AHK-um; sometimes spelled *Occam*) spent his entire career as a member of the church. A Franciscan monk (see entry on St. Francis), he taught at Oxford University and is most often associated with his writings on the nature of ideas.

Ockham reacted against Scholasticism, a philosophical movement that attempted to bring together Christian faith, classical learning, and knowledge of the world. Scholasticism had represented a great move of progress when it had its beginnings with **Abelard**, and by the time it reached its high point with **Thomas Aquinas** (see entries), it became a solidly entrenched way of thinking among Western European philosophers. Ockham helped bring about the end of Scholasticism and the beginnings of modern thought. He effectively ended a long-running Scholastic debate over the nature of ideas, holding that there is no such thing as a universal, only individuals—for instance, there is no perfect form of *red,* only numerous examples of red objects.

In forming this argument, Ockham maintained that "entities must not be unnecessarily multiplied." This, the famous "Ockham's razor," means that people should always seek the most simple and straightforward explanation for something. For example, if a man's cap falls off while he is sleeping, it is probably because he leaned forward in his sleep and it slid off—not because angels and demons got into a tug of war over his hat until one of them dropped it.

Clearly, Ockham's reasoning went against the grain of the medieval mind. So, too, did his political beliefs: if Anselm and Becket leaned too far to the side of the church, Ockham was equally strident in his support of secular power, particularly that of Holy Roman Emperor Ludwig IV. Ockham became involved in a dispute between the Franciscans and Pope John XXII, and was forced to flee the papal court at Avignon (AV-in-yawn) in France in 1328. Most of his writings during the last two decades of his life involved political attacks on the pope, and support for secular rulers.

Geoffrey Chaucer.

Geoffrey Chaucer

The career of Geoffrey Chaucer illustrated the transition from church power to secular power. Chaucer, known as "the father of English poetry" and the first widely celebrated writer in English, earned his living not as a priest or monk, but through the support or patronage of wealthy and powerful men such as the nobleman John of Gaunt. Chaucer's fortunes rose and fell with those of Gaunt and the royal house, including Gaunt's sons who became kings as Richard II and Henry IV.

Chaucer's first important work, *Book of the Duchess*, was written to comfort Gaunt following the death of his first wife, Blanche, in 1368. Later, in honor of Richard, he wrote *House of Fame* and *Parlement of Foules*. The former was said to have been influenced by **Dante** (see entry), and the latter was an allegory, or symbolic work of a type well known in the Middle Ages, discussing the nature of love. The spelling of the second title indicates that the English known to Chaucer is what today is referred to as Middle English, describing the period in the language's development between the Norman Invasion of 1066 and the invention of the printing press in the mid-1400s.

Adapting an earlier work by Giovanni Boccaccio (see box in Murasaki Shikibu entry), Chaucer wrote *Troylus and Criseyde* (KRES-i-duh), set during the Trojan War in ancient Greece. Chaucer's last work, however, was his masterpiece: the *Canterbury Tales*. Begun around 1386, the poem involves a group of travelers on their way to Becket's shrine at Canterbury. They represent a spectrum of medieval society, from a highly respected knight to various peasants, and each has a tale to tell. These tales, most of which are just as entertaining today as they were six centuries ago, represent a spectrum of medieval themes, including courtly love, allegory, and stories of instruction.

It was a measure of the respect with which Chaucer was viewed that following his death on October 25, 1400, he was buried at Westminster Abbey, a great church in London. The abbey had formerly been reserved for burial of royalty, but Chaucer was the first of many distinguished commoners buried there. The section where he was laid to rest came to be known as Poet's Corner, and later housed the remains of several highly admired English writers.

For More Information

Books

Corfe, Tom. *The Murder of Archbishop Thomas*. Minneapolis, MN: Lerner Publications, 1977.

Duggan, Alfred Leo. *The Falcon and the Dove: A Life of Thomas Becket of Canterbury*. Decorations by Anne Marie Jauss. New York: Pantheon Books, 1966.

McCaughrean, Geraldine, reteller. *The Canterbury Tales*. Illustrated by Victor G. Ambrus. New York: Oxford University Press, 1995.

Web Sites

"Alcuin (735–804) & Creative Quotations." *Be More Creative*. [Online] Available http://www.bemorecreative.com/one/1516.htm (last accessed July 26, 2000).

"Geoffreychaucer.org: An Annotated Guide to Online Resources." *Geoffreychaucer.org.* [Online] Available http://geoffreychaucer.org/ (last accessed July 26, 2000).

"Medieval Sourcebook: England." *Medieval Sourcebook.* [Online] Available http://www.fordham.edu/halsall/sbook1n.html (last accessed July 26, 2000).

"Ockham, William Of." [Online] Available http://www.cco.caltech.edu/~maronj/text/ockham.html (last accessed July 26, 2000).

"Thomas Becket." [Online] Available http://www.loyno.edu/~letchie/becket/ (last accessed July 26, 2000).

St. Francis of Assisi

Born 1182
Died 1226

Italian religious leader

Francis of Assisi is remembered as a great example of saint-hood as that term is understood both within the Catholic Church and by the world in general. As with **Augustine** (see entry), an encounter with God transformed him from a reckless youth to a sober, thoughtful defender of the faith. Unlike Augustine, however, Francis produced no significant writings: rather, his triumph was in his deeds for the poor and the needy. His kindness to all creatures and his belief that all deserved God's good will became legendary, and later, tales circulated of his preaching to the animals.

A spoiled boy

The eldest son of Pietro and Pica Bernardone was born with the name Giovanni, or John, in the central Italian city of Assisi (uh-SEE-see). His father, a wealthy cloth merchant, was away on business at the time, but as soon as Pietro returned, the family began calling the boy by the nickname Francesco, or Francis.

"Francis, go repair my house, which is falling in ruins."

Christ's words to him, as reported by Francis

Portrait: *Reproduced by permission of the Corbis Corporation.*

121

Francis was a spoiled child, doted on by his parents, and he took little interest in things that proved difficult. Thus he never excelled in school, and throughout his career had such a limited command of writing that he typically dictated his letters and signed them with a simple cross.

Yet he learned to speak Latin, the language of learning at the time, and French, then the language of international business. He also helped his father by cutting cloth in the latter's store, and it was said that he loved to flirt with the pretty young female customers.

Parties and wars

Francis grew up on dreams of glory, encouraged by his father, who wanted him to become a knight. In his teen years, however, he showed little of the discipline necessary for anyone who aspired to knighthood. Francis and his gang of friends, mostly wealthy youths who had plenty of money and time, were given to partying, practical jokes, and idleness. Like the others, he cared little for anything beyond the pleasures of the moment, but even then, Francis distinguished himself by his generosity, both to his friends and to the poor.

The teenaged Francis little suspected how soon his sheltered world would be destroyed. At that point, much of Italy was caught in a struggle with the Holy Roman Empire, a confederation of German principalities that controlled much of Europe, but in 1197, Assisi declared its independence. The foreign rulers of Assisi, loyal subjects of the empire, fled to the nearby town of Perugia, whose people had long been enemies of Assisi. In 1201, Perugia declared war on Assisi, and Francis was taken prisoner during the Battle of Ponte San Giovanni in November 1202.

He was held captive in Perugia for a year, during which time he began suffering health problems. Francis had always been weak, and his years of drinking and staying out late had only further weakened him; now confinement added to ailments that he would suffer throughout his life. At the age of twenty-two, he seemed like an old man, and he spent weeks in bed. When he could finally walk again, he found that something had changed.

A change of direction

The first thing Francis noticed was that all the things he had loved—partying, feasting, riding—no longer held the same pleasure for him that they once had. Still, he resolved to get on with the business of becoming a knight, and rode away to join the armies of Pope **Innocent III** (ruled 1198–1216; see entry) in their ongoing battles with the Holy Roman Empire.

On his way to join the army, Francis stopped overnight in the town of Spoleto (spoh-LAY-doh), where he had a dream. In it, God asked him which lord he would serve: an earthly lord or commander in the army, or the Lord God in Heaven. Francis was so moved that he returned to Assisi.

At home, people dubbed him a coward, and his parents were puzzled and embarrassed by Francis's behavior. All his old friends were away at war, and he began spending long hours praying in churches around the town. In 1206, he was kneeling at the Chapel of San Damiano when he heard what he believed was the voice of Christ saying to him: "Francis, go repair my house, which is falling in ruins."

In the aftermath of this strange experience, Francis renounced worldly riches and began begging in the streets. By this he hoped to raise funds to restore churches such as San Damiano, which was clearly in need of repair. But he was also begging to support himself, and his father was mortified by his behavior. In April 1207, he had Francis brought before a magistrate or judge, who he hoped would order him to stop begging, go home, and start living in a way appropriate to his upbringing.

Francis requested that his hearing occur before a bishop, to which the father agreed, and in the bishop's presence the young man stripped off his clothing and announced: "I have called Pietro Bernardone my father…. Now I will say Our Father who art in heaven, not Pietro Bernardone." Thus he renounced his old life, and began a new one.

The start of the Franciscans

Up to this point, Francis still believed that God wanted him to literally repair churches, but in the follow-

St. Dominic

Not only was St. Dominic (c. 1170–1221) almost an exact contemporary of St. Francis, but he too established a mendicant order of friars—that is, preachers and teachers who lived on alms or donations. Unlike Francis, however, Dominic seems to have been a devout follower of Christ even from his early years as a boy in Spain.

In Spain at that time, the Christian north was locked in a struggle against the Muslim south. As a result of the war, famine broke out in the town of Palencia, where the teenaged Dominic was studying for the priesthood. He was enraged by the unwillingness of the wealthy to help the poor, and sold all his possessions to feed the hungry.

In his mid-twenties, Dominic became a priest in the town of Osma, and there began a lifelong friendship with the bishop Diego. The king of Castile (kas-TEEL), the dominant Christian region in Spain, sent the two men to Rome on a diplomatic mission, and on their way through southern France, they were astounded by the differences between that region and their homeland.

Because of the struggle with the Muslims, the Christians of Spain were serious about their faith, whereas in southern France the priests had given in to lives of pleasure. The most devoted believers seemed to be the heretics, or people who

ing year he came to realize that his mission was one of repairing people's hearts—of fixing the church on the inside, in places that could not be seen. He began to model his life on that of Christ, as told in the Gospels from the New Testament; therefore he wandered the land, preaching, caring for the sick, and maintaining little in the way of material possessions.

At that time there were many wandering preachers, men who thundered about God's wrath, or the coming judgment of the world, or even about a particular leader who they claimed would be struck down by God. Francis's message was different: like Christ, he taught about God's love, and soon he attracted many followers.

In time, there were people who not only wanted to hear his message, but many who sought to live as Francis did. Thus was born the Franciscan order, a group of friars (preachers and teachers). In order to establish this order, however, had adopted beliefs that went against established church teachings. Chief among the heretical groups were the Cathars, sometimes known as the Albigenses (al-buh-JIN-seez).

The typical response of the church to heresy was condemnation and punishment, but Dominic took a different approach. Moved by what he saw as their misguided faith, he sought to reason with the Cathars, and persuade them of their errors. For some time, he made considerable progress in his efforts at conversion, but two occurences doomed his mission. First was the death of Diego, who he had depended upon in his efforts; then, in 1208,

the murder of a church official in the area sparked the Albigensian Crusade, a "holy war" against the region. The result was slaughter and mayhem, and Dominic returned to Spain in disgust.

All was not lost, however: Dominic attracted a group of friars around him, and in 1215 was granted permission to start the Dominican Order. As with the Franciscans, the Dominicans included women, in separate orders of nuns. In the last six years of Dominic's life, the order spread throughout Europe; and in the 1500s, Spanish exploration spread the Dominican influence to East Asia and the Americas.

Francis had to get the pope's approval, and at first Innocent refused. After meeting with Francis, however, the pope himself had a strange dream.

In it, he saw the Church of St. John Lateran, the principal church in Rome, start to tilt over and fall; then suddenly a man in rags—who Innocent recognized as Francis—caught it and saved it. The pope approved the establishment of the Franciscan order, and in 1223 he authorized it as a Rule, a group under which other orders were established.

An inclusive message

As was the case with St. Dominic (see box), the order established by Francis had a place for women. An early follower was Clare of Assisi, member of a noble family, who ran away from home with her cousin Pacifica. They went to Francis, who cut off their hair and gave them clothes of rough material, a symbol that they renounced the things of the world. Joined later by Clare's younger sister Agnes, the three nuns developed an order known as the "Poor Clares."

Clearly Francis's message was one that included rather than excluded people. Although stories about him preaching to the animals are almost certainly legendary, they help to symbolize the fact that he believed God's love was for everyone. He even tried to travel to the Holy Land and to Morocco, where Christians were engaged in crusades against Muslims, in hopes of ending the fighting. This was a rare viewpoint for his time, when most Christians in Western Europe regarded such "holy wars" as service to God. Unfortunately, Francis's health and other problems prevented him from making those journeys.

In his latter years, Francis saw the order he had established grow in numbers, but it lost something in its growth. Francis had intended his group to be small, composed of men and women willing to undergo the utmost in hardship; but as the movement grew, its standards were lowered to accommodate more people.

A legendary figure

Seeking to separate himself from the hustle and bustle of the world, Francis went on a pilgrimage to the mountain of La Verda, north of Assisi. It was there, according to legend, that he received the stigmata—nail marks on his hands and feet, and a wound in his side. The stigmata was a phenomenon said to occur to the most devout, and the wounds exactly replicated those Christ had suffered during his crucifixion.

Poor health brought an early end to Francis's life, at the age of forty-four. Another tale about him held that in death, his body was renewed: his skin became white, and his face lost all signs of aging, while the wounds of Christ turned black. Whatever the truth of these claims, they attested to the legendary status he had already acquired within his lifetime. Just two years after his death—an extremely short interval—he was canonized, or declared a saint.

For More Information

Books

Bunson, Margaret and Matthew. *St. Francis of Assisi.* Huntington, IN: Our Sunday Visitor, 1992.

Mayo, Margaret. *Brother Sun, Sister Moon: The Life and Stories of St. Francis.* Illustrated by Peter Malone. Boston: Little, Brown, and Company, 2000.

Wildsmith, Brian. *Saint Francis.* Grand Rapids, MI: William B. Eerdmans Publishing Company, 1996.

Motion Pictures

Francis of Assisi. Twentieth Century Fox, 1961.

Web Sites

"St. Dominic and His Life." [Online] Available http://www.op.org/domcentral/trad/stdom.htm (last accessed July 26, 2000).

"St. Francis of Assisi." [Online] Available http://www.cyberenet.net/~kelta/stfrancis.html (last accessed July 26, 2000).

Genghis Khan

Born c. 1162
Died 1227

Mongolian chieftain and conqueror

No empire in history has ever been as large as that conquered in the 1200s by the Mongols, who began their conquests as a simple nation of shepherds and nomads in Central Asia. What welded them into a mighty fighting force was not a religion, or a political belief, or even a shared need for land or food; it was a man, a severe but shrewd warlord known to history as Genghis Khan.

The son of a chieftain

Today Mongolia is a quiet, underpopulated, and underdeveloped land to the north of China. For centuries, it had been home to a hardy nomadic people who had no written language or—until the Middle Ages—cities of their own. The man who briefly made Mongolia the most powerful nation on Earth was born with the name Temujin (TIM-yuh-jin) in 1162.

According to legend, Temujin came into the world grasping a lump of clotted blood, a sign of the forcefulness and violence that would dominate his life. His father was a chieftain

> "A man's greatest work is to break his enemies, to drive them before him, to take from them all the things that have been theirs."

Portrait.

named Yesugei (YES-oo-gay), who, when the boy was still young, arranged his marriage to Borte (BOHR-tuh), the daughter of a neighboring chieftain. The families celebrated with a feast, but while returning to his clan's area, Yesugei was poisoned by Tatars (TAT-arz), another nomadic group in the region.

A harsh childhood

Not only was Temujin's mother Ho'elun (hoh-LOON) left a widow and her children fatherless, but the status of nine-year-old Temujin, his father's designated heir, was uncertain. When the leader of another clan, Targutai (tar-goo-TY), seized all their possessions, Temujin's family was defenseless. They might have died had it not been for the resourcefulness and determination of his mother.

Over the next five years, Ho'elun kept her family— Temujin, a younger brother, two older half-brothers, and other smaller children—alive by avoiding the areas controlled by Targutai. This meant that they had to live off of the worst hunting and grazing grounds, and many times they barely made it through a winter without starving. The experience was unquestionably a hardening one for Temujin, who no doubt grew up quickly in the harsh environment of the Central Asia steppes (pronounced "steps"; vast areas of arid land with few or no trees).

When Temujin was fourteen, Targutai learned that he was still alive, and ordered his capture. Temujin managed to escape from a wooden harness in which his captors confined him, and taking advantage of their drunkenness during a feast, he fled their camp and returned to his family. The people who helped him in his escape, and the young men who joined forces with him immediately afterward, would later have honored places in his army. From among their ranks would come several of the hard-driving generals later referred to with admiration as the "Four Coursers of Genghis Khan."

Building his army

Steadily Temujin began taking what had been promised to him long before, and in due course he married

Mongol warriors gathering for battle. *Reproduced by permission of the Corbis Corporation.*

Borte. In honor of their marriage, his new father-in-law gave him a special cloak, and Temujin quickly gave the cloak as a present to Toghrul (tohg-ROOL), a powerful chieftain who had once been an ally of his father's. In the Mongolian culture, which placed a strong emphasis on honoring those more powerful, it was an extremely wise move.

Thus when Borte was kidnapped by a band of enemy tribesmen, Temujin was able to call on the aid of Toghrul. He also asked the help of a childhood friend named Jamukha, and their three forces—Temujin hastily raised an army of his own—defeated the enemy tribe and rescued Borte. For some time after this, Temujin and Jamukha were the closest of friends, but for some reason they later parted ways. Shortly after Jamukha and his men left Temujin's camp, in 1187, a group of clans proclaimed Temujin "Genghis Khan" (JING-us KAHN), meaning "rightful ruler."

Brian Boru

There is no historical indication that Brian Boru (buh-ROO; c. 941–1014), king of Ireland, had any of the cruel ways typically attributed to Genghis Khan; nonetheless, there were similarities between the two men, though they were widely separated by time and space. Both grew up hiding from enemies, surrounded by a nation disunited and given to internal quarrels, and both would later unite their people and lead them to victory. The empire won by Genghis barely outlasted his grandchildren; Brian's united Ireland did not outlast his own lifetime.

Brian's father led one of several kingdoms that constituted Ireland, and though the Irish had a single "high king," the position lacked any real authority to unite the nation. This made them vulnerable to attacks from outsiders, and in Brian's time Ireland was under constant threat from the Danes, descendants of the Vikings. Together with his older brother and others, Brian waged a long war against the Danes. Later, however, his brother tired of fighting and agreed to make peace with the enemy, but Brian refused to so, and continued fighting.

Eventually Brian won over enough kingdoms to pose a serious challenge to the Danes, and he set out to conquer all of Ireland. In 999, he won the capital city of Dublin, and in 1002 became high king. Now more than sixty years old, he turned his attention from battle to administration, seeking to solidify the position of the high

Betrayed by old allies

Despite his impressive title, Genghis was but one of several khans, or chieftains, and in the years that followed, tensions between him and other leaders—particularly Jamukha—would grow. In 1198, both men aided the Chinese in a successful war against a common enemy, the Tatars. The shared effort, however, did little to reunite Genghis and Jamukha, and in 1191, clans opposed to Genghis's leadership recognized Jamukha as Gur Khan, or "sole ruler." They then launched an attack against Genghis, who managed to ward them off with the aid of Toghrul's troops.

In 1203, however, Jamukha influenced Toghrul to join his side, and they plotted to double-cross Genghis. Once again, the celebration of a betrothal—that is, the promise of a marriage, in this case of Toghrul's son to Genghis's daugh-

Brian Boru. *Reproduced by permission of Archive Photos, Inc.*

king. He also formed a strong alliance with the Catholic Church, and instituted a system of church schools to strengthen education throughout the country.

In later years, Brian referred to himself as "emperor of the Irish," and seems to have consciously modeled his rule on that of **Charlemagne** (see entry) and other great European figures. Though he had authority over the other kings of Ireland, many opposed his power. Eventually his enemies formed an alliance with the Danes, and marched against Brian on Good Friday, April 23, 1014. Brian was killed, and though ironically his side won the battle, their cause was lost without their leader. Brian's vision of Irish unity died with him.

ter—would provide the occasion for the betrayal. Toghrul's son tried to lure Genghis to a feast, where they would kill him, but one of Genghis's advisors figured out what was going on, and urged him not to go.

Genghis gathered his forces, and called on the clans that had sworn their allegiance to him, but they doubted his ability to win against the superior forces of his enemies, so they chose to stay out of the battle. That battle was inconclusive, but soon afterward, Genghis defeated Toghrul. Next came Jamukha, who he captured some months later. Reportedly Genghis offered his old friend the opportunity to let bygones be bygones, but Jamukha was supposedly so ashamed at his capture that he demanded to be killed. Whether or not this is true, Genghis's men killed him, and in 1206 the Mongols united as a nation for the first time and proclaimed Genghis "ruler of all men."

Conquering China

With a swift and sudden fury, Genghis—then about forty-four years old—rode onto the pages of history, leaving an indelible mark in the twenty-one years that remained for him. The reasons behind his conquest of such a large empire are not clear, but it seems as though he simply started going and never stopped. The Mongols were extraordinarily fierce warriors who struck terror in the hearts of their victims, a terror that was justified by the heaps of corpses they left behind them. It simply did not occur to Genghis to let people live: in his mind, leaving survivors would require him to devote troops to overseeing them, and he wanted to keep on moving.

His viewpoint on conquered peoples began to change somewhat when, in 1211, after subduing several other peoples along the Chinese border, he and his armies went after China itself. The Chinese had long regarded the Mongols as just one of many "barbarian" groups at the fringes of their empire, and had believed that the Mongols' rightful place was as servants to China. Now that was about to change. By 1215, Genghis's hordes, as the Mongol troops were called, had reached Peking, now more commonly known as Beijing (bay-ZHEENG; capital of modern China), which they virtually destroyed. Soon afterward, a former official of the Chinese emperor pointed out to Genghis that if he allowed some people to continue living in the lands he conquered, they could pay him valuable tax money to finance further warfare. Genghis accepted this sound advice, and changed his tactics in the future.

The conquest of the world

In 1216, a sultan in Persia unwisely offended Genghis, who sent his troops westward to take what is now Iran, Afghanistan, southern Russia, Georgia, and Armenia. By 1223, the Mongols controlled a region that stretched from the borders of Turkey to northern India to China.

Genghis himself, about sixty-five years old, died on August 18, 1227, of complications resulting from falling off a horse. He was buried in northeastern Mongolia, and it was said that forty beautiful maidens and forty horses were slaughtered before his grave.

In the years that followed Genghis's death, the Mongolian empire would grow to reach from the outskirts of Vienna, Austria, in the west, to the Korean Peninsula in the east. It was an almost unbelievably vast realm, and the driving force behind its conquest had been Genghis. Within less than two centuries, the Mongols' empire would fade into memory, and the Mongols themselves would retreat to their homeland.

For More Information

Books

Brill, Marlene Targ. *Extraordinary Young People.* New York: Children's Press, 1996.

Demi. *Chinghis Khan.* New York: H. Holt, 1991.

Encyclopedia of World Biography, second edition. Detroit: Gale, 1998.

Lamb, Harold. *Genghis Khan and the Mongol Horde.* Illustrated by Elton Fax. Hamden, CT: Linnet Books, 1990.

Langley, Andrew. *100 Greatest Tyrants.* Danbury, CT: Grolier Educational, 1997.

Web Sites

"Bios: Genghis Khan." [Online] Available http://library.thinkquest.org/17120/data/bios/khan/ (last accessed July 26, 2000).

"Boru." [Online] Available http://www.irishstoryteller.com/boru.html (last accessed July 26, 2000).

"Brian Boru." *Clannada na Gadelica.* [Online] Available http://www.clannada.org/docs/brianboru.htm (last accessed July 26, 2000).

"Empires beyond the Great Wall: The Heritage of Genghis Khan." [Online] Available http://vvv.com:80/khan/index.html (last accessed July 26, 2000).

"The History of Ireland—Irish Royalty." [Online] Available http://www.geocities.com/Athens/Aegean/7545/Ireland.html (last accessed July 26, 2000).

"P.M.A.: Virtual Exhibits—Genghis Khan." *Provincial Museum of Alberta.* [Online] Available http://www.pma.edmonton.ab.ca/vexhibit/genghis/intro.htm (last accessed July 26, 2000).

Gregory I
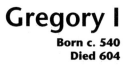
Born c. 540
Died 604

Italian pope

When Gregory I, or Gregory the Great, became pope in 590, the church and indeed all of Western Europe was in ruins. People still believed that the Western Roman Empire, smashed by barbarian invasions more than a century before, could be resurrected with the help of the Eastern Roman Empire in Greece. Gregory himself started out with that belief, but when he got no help from the emperor in Constantinople, he began building the church as a powerful, self-sufficient political entity.

A Roman prefect

As with many figures from the premodern period, little is known about Gregory's early life. He was born in about 540, a member of a wealthy Roman family. The family enjoyed great political power as well, but the Rome they lived in was a mere shadow of its former glory: two centuries of destruction by barbarian tribes such as the Lombards had left it in ruins. This ruining of Rome was both physical, in terms of the buildings and structures, and spiritual. The old laws of

"I have taken charge of an old and grievously shattered ship."

On becoming pope

Portrait: *Reproduced by permission of the Granger Collection Ltd.*

Roman society had broken down, and along with them the order that had made Rome a great empire many years before.

Yet Rome retained some of the trappings of its former life, including the office of prefect, a magistrate or judge. Gregory, after receiving a classical education—his was one of the last generations of Romans to have access to the old-fashioned learning that had produced so many well-educated Romans in the past—became prefect in 573. This might have been enough for some men, but Gregory had his eyes on higher things.

A monk forced into politics

From an early age, Gregory had been a strongly committed Christian, and in his thirties he became interested in the life of a monk. Monks separated themselves from the rest of society to pray, meditate, and work, often under severe conditions, in monasteries. At first Gregory was content to establish monasteries for others: he set up one in Rome and six more on lands owned by his family in Sicily, an island to the south of Italy. But some time around 574 or 575, he decided to leave the outside world and become a monk himself.

After six years of living in a monastery, sharing hardships with the other monks, Gregory was given a job by Pope Gelasius II. Recognizing Gregory's training and ability, the pope asked him to go to the imperial court in Constantinople and plead with the emperor there for troops and supplies to help defend Rome against another wave of Lombard invasions. Thus Gregory was forced to leave the monastery and enter the realm of politics.

The mission to Constantinople proved fruitless, but in the meantime Gregory had attracted the attention of church leaders. As a result, when Gelasius died in 590, they chose Gregory as his successor.

Gregory's world

The term "world," as used in the Christian religion, does not necessarily mean the planet Earth, or the nations of the world; rather, "worldly" is the opposite of "godly." In a tradition that went back at least to **Augustine** (see entry), Christians considered things of the world—even things such as earning a living, which few people believed to be morally bad—as less important than things of the spirit.

Gregory would spend his entire career torn between the sacred and the *secular,* which comes from a Latin word meaning "world." As a monk, he favored a regimen of austerity, sleeping on hard beds, eating and sleeping little, and focusing his attention on God. However, as bishop of Rome, or pope, he had to be concerned with matters such as protecting and feeding the people under his charge.

The hardships Gregory forced on himself made him physically weak throughout his reign as pope, a fact that makes his accomplishments all the more great. Gregory is remembered as one of four "Doctors of the Church," or church fathers, along with Augustine, Ambrose (339–397), and Jerome (c. 347–c. 419). The other three were roughly contemporaries of each other, all living at a time when the Western Roman Empire was entering its final decline. Yet Gregory's era, some 250 years later, was an even more frightening time.

In the year he became pope, there was a famine and flood in Rome, as well as a plague in various parts of Europe. Gregory and other Christians took such events as evidence that the world was coming to an end, and for support they pointed to passages in the New Testament that seemed to say the end would be sooner rather than later. Thus he felt a sense of mission to bring as many people as possible into the Christian fold before Christ returned to judge the world, as predicted in the Bible.

A strong pope

With his sense of urgency concerning the end of the world, Gregory was able to marshal his weakened body to enormous feats of energy. He left behind some eight hundred letters, along with several books, and these attest to a highly complex, energetic man with an iron will. The people of Western Europe needed just such a figure to lead them.

It is thanks to Gregory that the pope became the leader of Western Christianity. In his time, a number of other bishops

Boniface VIII

If Gregory represented the beginnings of popes' great political power during the Middle Ages, Boniface VIII (BAHN-i-fus; c. 1235–1303; ruled 1294–1303) seven centuries later symbolized the end of that power. Born Benedict Caetani (kah-ay-TAHN-ee), he was the son of wealthy parents in Anagni (ah-NAHN-yee), a town in central Italy. He studied law, but by the age of thirty had begun a career in the church as secretary to Cardinal Simon of Brie. When the latter became Pope Martin IV in 1281, he made Benedict a cardinal.

Thanks to gifts both by kings and a series of popes, Benedict became wealthy as well as powerful during his time as cardinal. Meanwhile a struggle raged between different political groups eager to win control of the papacy. It took them more than two years after the death of Nicholas IV in 1292 to choose a successor, and when they did it was a highly unlikely candidate: a her-

mit named Peter of Morrone, who became Pope Celestine V. Peter had no desire to be pope, and resigned after four months. Later, critics would charge that Benedict had urged the resignation; whatever the case, he now became pope as Boniface VIII.

Popes and kings had long been locked in a struggle for power, and Boniface set out to show his superiority over the kings of France and England by stating that his priests had no obligation to pay taxes to their governments. Boniface wanted the priests to pay taxes to *him,* just as all kings were supposed to pay taxes to the pope. The response was one of anger, particularly from King Philip IV of France, who refused to pay any taxes at all. Boniface backed down in 1297, saying that priests should make "gifts" to monarchs in times of emergency.

In 1301, Philip had a French bishop arrested for a variety of crimes, includ-

vied with the bishop of Rome for supremacy. There was the bishop of Constantinople, whose office, renamed "patriarch," would become the leading position in the Greek Orthodox Church after the split with the Roman Catholic Church in 1054. There were also bishops in Jerusalem, the city where Jesus had walked; in Antioch, an early Christian stronghold in what is now Syria; and Alexandria, an Egyptian center of Greek culture.

Gregory, however, believed that there was a biblical basis for the bishop of Rome assuming leadership. Once again he tried to receive help from the emperor of the Eastern Roman Empire, or Byzantine Empire; but Emperor Maurice

Pope Boniface VIII. *Reproduced by permission of the Library of Congress.*

ed a smear campaign against Boniface, including charges that he had arranged the murder of Celestine V, who had died earlier. Boniface issued a decree called *Unam Sanctum* in which he stated that the pope held the keys to eternal salvation, and was therefore *the* leader of all Christian society.

Just how much power Boniface really had became apparent when Philip arranged to have him condemned by a number of French church leaders in 1303, then sent soldiers to arrest the pope. Philip only imprisoned Boniface for two days, from September 7 to 9, but in those two days history was changed. Never again would popes rule as unquestioned leaders of Europe, and from that point on, the power of kings grew while the power of the papacy slowly faded. Boniface died five weeks later, on October 12, defeated and humiliated.

ing treason, and asked Boniface to remove the man from his office. Boniface refused, and revoked all the privileges that the French king enjoyed in the way of influencing church affairs. Philip start-

turned a deaf ear to his requests that Maurice recognize his leadership in the church. Later, Maurice was murdered by one of his generals, but Gregory in the meantime had decided that he could lead the Christians of Italy with or without the help of the emperor.

The foundations of medieval politics

Gregory's decision formed the cornerstone of medieval politics: instead of relying on a king to protect against the Lombards, or to distribute grain in times of famine, Gregory took on the job himself. Thus the papacy became a political as well as a spiritual office. The power of the popes would rise to staggering heights in centuries to come, and it could all be traced back to Gregory—yet Gregory did what he did, not because he wanted power, but because he felt there was no choice.

During his extraordinarily active career, Gregory ransomed prisoners and constantly welcomed refugees from war-torn Italy into the relatively safe confines of Rome. He took power over corrupt bishops who were buying and selling church offices (a sin known as simony), committing adultery, and doing other things inappropriate to their roles as spiritual leaders. He dealt harshly with heresy, or behavior that went against church doctrine, yet often negotiated with Lombard leaders who still embraced the heretical branch of Christianity called Arianism. He constantly promoted the purity of the monastic lifestyle and tried to keep the church free from worldly corruption; yet he built up its political power to such a degree that corruption was bound to seep in.

Among Gregory's achievements were the conversion to Catholic Christianity of the Lombards from the Arian heresy, and of the Anglo-Saxons from paganism. The conversion of the English took place under Augustine of Canterbury (died 604), who Gregory sent to Britain. Augustine became the first archbishop of Canterbury, the religious leader of Britain. Gregory also showed his ability to negotiate with the Franks in France, and the Visigoths in Spain, even though neither of these groups formally accepted the leadership of the pope.

Gregory's effect could be observed throughout Europe, from the haunting tones of Gregorian chants—a type of singing performed by Benedictine monks, written down for future generations under his orders—to the many tales of miracles associated with him and with his death in 604. Yet his greatest legacy was in the formation of the church as a political power, and of Western Europe or Christendom as a political and spiritual alliance united under the leadership of a strong pope.

For More Information

Books

McDonald, Father Stephen James. *Bible History with a History of the Church*. New York: Row, Peterson and Company, 1940.

Rice, Edward. *A Young People's Pictorial History of the Church.* Text adapted by Blanche Jennings Thompson. New York: Farrar, Straus, 1963.

Sanderlin, George William. *St. Gregory the Great, Consul of God.* New York: Vision Books, 1964.

Web Sites

Brusher, the Rev. Joseph, S. J. "Popes through the Ages." [Online] Available http://www.ewtn.com/library/CHRIST/POPES.TXT (last accessed July 26, 2000).

"Catholic Encyclopedia: List of Popes." *Catholic Encyclopedia.* [Online] Available http://www.newadvent.org/cathen/12272b.htm (last accessed July 26, 2000).

"Chronology of Pope Gregory the Great." [Online] Available http://members.aol.com/butrousch/augustine/gregory.htm (last accessed July 26, 2000).

"Chronology of Popes." *Information Please.* [Online] Available http://looksmart.infoplease.com/ce5/CE039386.html (last accessed July 26, 2000).

"Pope Saint Gregory the Great." [Online] Available http://www.iea.com/~bradh/popes/pope_chapter2.htm (last accessed July 26, 2000).

Gregory VII

Born c. 1020
Died 1085

Italian pope

Henry IV

Born 1050
Died 1106

German king and Holy Roman emperor

Gregory VII was the pope, leader of the Catholic Church, and Henry IV, as Holy Roman emperor, ruled a number of lands. Thus they were the two most powerful men in Western Europe, and in 1075, they faced off in a power struggle called the Investiture Controversy that would have an enormous impact on history.

The immediate cause was the right of the emperors to appoint bishops and other church leaders, a right that the pope claimed solely for himself. In reality, the conflict between Gregory and Henry represented a much larger battle between church and state, a battle that would influence events in the Middle Ages and would continue to affect public life even in modern times.

Gregory's early years

The future Pope Gregory VII was born with the name Hildebrand in Rovaca, a village in northern Italy, in about 1020. In medieval Europe, it was not uncommon for a young

> "In the name of Almighty God, Father, Son and Holy Ghost, I withdraw ... from Henry ... the rule over the whole kingdom of the Germans and over Italy. And I absolve all Christians from the bonds of the oath which they have made or shall make to him; and I forbid any one to serve him as king."
>
> *"First Deposition and Banning of Henry IV," February 22, 1076*

man to know—or rather, to be told—what he would do for a living when he was still very young. Thus as a boy Hildebrand began an education for the priesthood, and later became a monk in the Benedictine order.

Hildebrand underwent much of his education in Rome, center of the Catholic Church and home of the pope. In 1032, Benedict IX had become pope, but with his loose lifestyle and riotous living, he became unpopular, and was overthrown twelve years later. Benedict managed to return to the papal throne, however, for a short time before selling his position to the future Pope Gregory VI.

The fact that someone could sell off the papal throne, which was supposed to be sacred before God, said much about the state of affairs in the Catholic Church at the time. As pope, Hildebrand would do much to reform the church, yet he got his start in papal affairs by serving as chaplain to Gregory VI from 1045 to 1047.

Emperors and popes

Centuries earlier, Pope Leo III had crowned **Charlemagne** (see entry) as "Emperor of the Romans." From this title had arisen the idea of the Holy Roman Empire, which comprised a number of small states in what is now Germany and surrounding countries. Though the empire was seldom a strongly unified realm, the title of emperor had great symbolic status for German kings, who were usually crowned at special ceremonies in Rome.

In 1046, three men—Benedict, Gregory VI, and Sylvester III, who had briefly occupied the throne after Benedict—all claimed the papal throne. King Henry III of Germany, father of Henry IV, traveled to Italy to straighten out the situation. His solution was to remove all three and install a new pope, Clement II, who crowned him emperor.

Gregory VI was forced into exile in Germany, and he took Hildebrand with him. Two years later, however, in 1049, Hildebrand returned to Rome as advisor to Pope Leo IX, and over the years that followed, he would occupy a number of important positions within the church.

Henry's early years

When Hildebrand was thirty years old, his future rival Henry IV was born in Germany. Not long afterward, in 1056, Henry III died, and therefore his six-year-old son became king of Germany. Until he reached the age of sixteen, however, Henry's mother Agnes of Poitou (pwah-TÜ) ruled in his place as regent.

In the early years of his reign, Henry fought a series of conflicts with nobles—rulers within his kingdom who had inherited title and lands, but held less power than the king—from the German region of Saxony. In 1075, however, the twenty-five-year-old king would face the most powerful opponent of his life: Pope Gregory VII.

Pope Gregory VII was determined to rid the church of corruption and increase the power of the papacy, which resulted in a historic confrontation with Emperor Henry IV.
Reproduced by permission of the Corbis Corporation.

Gregory the reformer

On April 21, 1073, Pope Alexander II died. Soon afterward Hildebrand, who had become immensely popular among the people of Rome, was elected pope by the cardinals, the highest officials within the church other than the pope himself. In honor of Gregory VI, he chose the title Gregory VII.

Gregory set about reforming the church, which had long been in decline. Not only could church offices be bought and sold, but increasingly more corrupt men had taken positions of power, thus weakening the moral authority of the pope and other church leaders. With the church in a shambles, Gregory was determined to put it back on the right course—and to show the Holy Roman emperor who was boss.

For many years, emperors had been investing, or appointing, bishops within the church. On February 24, 1075, however, Gregory issued orders banning lay investiture, or appointment of bishops by leaders outside the church. Not long afterward, he put down on paper a list of twenty-seven key points about the papacy, or the office of the pope: for instance,

Matilda of Tuscany

Though she was related to Emperor Henry IV, Matilda of Tuscany (c. 1046–1115) took part in the Investiture Controversy on the side of Pope Gregory VII. Her family had long controlled lands in northern Italy, including Canossa, site of the castle where Gregory and Henry had an important meeting in 1077.

Matilda was raised in an unconventional way for a young girl of the Middle Ages, receiving the sort of comprehensive and wide-ranging education that was normally set aside only for boys. Clearly she was being groomed for leadership, and upon the death of her father and brother in 1052, Matilda became countess of Tuscany.

Knowing that neighboring princes might want to invade a region "ruled" by a six-year-old girl, her mother married Godfrey, duke of Lorraine (a region on the border between France and Germany.) However, Godfrey was in conflict with Emperor Henry III of Germany, who imprisoned both mother and daughter from 1055 to 1056.

No doubt as a result of this experience, Matilda was no supporter of her German cousins. Furthermore, she became closely involved in church affairs, and her family were close friends with the future Pope Gregory VII. Therefore when the Investiture Controversy between Henry IV and Gregory VII came to a head, Matilda sided with Gregory. Nonetheless, the fact that she was related to Henry made her a natural go-between for the two opposing sides.

he wrote that no one had the right to question the pope's actions, and that kings and princes should kiss the pope's feet.

The conflict begins

In June 1075, Henry won a victory over the rebellious German princes with the help of his cousin Rudolf, duke of the German region of Swabia. He recognized that the German nobles wanted to challenge his power and would encourage a conflict between the pope and himself. He relayed this information to the pope, but in November 1076, he appointed a high church official himself in direct violation of the pope's order. This resulted in a letter from Gregory that threatened Henry's excommunication, or removal from the church.

Matilda of Tuscany. *Reproduced by permission of the Library of Congress.*

Like her mother before her, Matilda had sought to strengthen her position through marriage, in her case to her step-brother Godfrey the Hunchback in 1069. The purpose of this marriage was political, and after her infant son died in 1071, she returned to Italy. Godfrey died in 1076, but she remarried in 1089, once again for political reasons. This time the groom was Welf V, a German duke who supported the new pope, Victor III, against Henry. By this time she was forty-three, and Welf only seventeen.

Matilda enjoyed a much closer relationship with Henry V, son of Henry IV, than she had with his father. But when she died in 1115, leaving no heirs, Henry V claimed most of her lands. She was later celebrated in a long poem by Donizo, her chaplain at Canossa.

Angered by the pope's letter, in January 1076 Henry called together twenty-four bishops in the German city of Worms (VURMZ), and they sent a letter of protest to the pope. Along with this letter, Henry sent one of his own that called the pope "a false monk." This in turn enraged Gregory, who on February 22 issued orders declaring that Henry was excommunicated and damned to hell; furthermore, the people of his kingdom were forbidden from submitting to him.

The snows of Canossa

This put Henry in a very serious position, since medieval people were far more likely to follow the pope than they were a king. Rudolf took advantage of the situation to turn against Henry and gather support. Henry sent a message to the pope in which he offered to submit, but by then the pope had realized what the German nobles already knew: that if he allowed Henry to submit to him and thereby called off the fight, he would lose influence in Germany.

Henry went south, hoping to meet with Gregory, but he found his way blocked by nobles who wanted to prevent the meeting. Finally, in January 1077, he managed to cross the Alps, a high range of mountains between Germany and Italy. He arrived on January 25 at the pope's temporary residence, a castle belonging to Matilda of Tuscany (see box) at Canossa (kuh-NAH-suh) in northern Italy.

Barefoot and dressed in rags to indicate the fact that he had humbled himself before the pope's spiritual authority, Henry waited in the snow outside the castle. To test the king's sincerity, Gregory allowed him to remain outside in the cold for three whole days; then he agreed to forgive him, and ended his excommunication.

A change of fortunes

The scene at Canossa made for great drama; however, it was not the end of the story. On March 26, 1077, Rudolf declared himself king of Germany, and Rudolf and Henry began warring with each other for the throne. Henry demanded that Gregory help him by excommunicating Rudolf. Gregory, however, was more inclined to support Rudolf. When the war began to go in Henry's favor, Gregory declined to excommunicate Rudolf and instead re-excommunicated Henry.

This resulted in a war of words between church and state, or pope and king, and both enlisted the help of learned men who referred to the Bible on the one hand, or Roman law on the other, to prove that their leader should rule Europe. Henry even tried to replace Gregory with an antipope (someone not recognized as a true pope by the church), Clement III. The death of Rudolf in October 1080 helped him immensely, and he crushed all further resistance to his rule. By the early 1080s, he was on the offensive against the pope.

By 1083, Henry had captured the part of Rome that included the papal residence at St. Peter's, and he imprisoned

Gregory. On March 21, 1084, Henry won control over most of the city, and soon afterward placed Clement III on the papal throne. Clement in turn crowned Henry Holy Roman emperor, and excommunicated Gregory.

A painful ending

Now desperate, Gregory called on the help of Robert Guiscard (gee-SKARD), leader of a powerful Norman family that controlled the island of Sicily. Robert's forces marched on Rome and drove out Henry's army, but when the Romans resisted them, the Normans looted and burned much of the city. This in turn made Gregory a very unpopular man, and he fled Rome under the protection of the Normans.

Gregory died in exile soon afterward, on May 25, 1085. Henry went on living for twenty-one more years, but his life would end as painfully as Gregory's had. In 1093, his sons rebelled against him, and in 1105 one of them had him imprisoned. Henry escaped, but died soon afterward.

Church and state

In 1088, Urban II (see box in Innocent III entry), who had inherited Gregory's enthusiasm for papal authority, became pope. Seven years later, while Henry was caught up in struggles with his sons, Urban launched the First Crusade, a war to recapture the Holy Land from the Muslims who controlled it. In so doing, he greatly built up the authority of the popes over political leaders.

Henry's son Henry V, who had imprisoned his father, later reached an agreement with Pope Calixtus II in the Concordat of Worms (1122). The latter recognized the power of the popes, who for the next three centuries would remain among the most powerful leaders in Western Europe.

But popes would not rule without challenges from kings, who eventually gained more control. Even today, the struggle between church and state—that is, between the authority of government and that of religion—continues. In most Western countries, however, the political power is clearly in the hands of the government.

For More Information

Books

Cowdrey, H. E. J. *Pope Gregory VII, 1073–1085.* New York: Oxford University Press, 1998.

Dijkstra, Henk, editor. *History of the Ancient & Medieval World,* Volume 9: *The Middle Ages.* New York: Marshall Cavendish, 1996.

Fraser, Antonio. *Boadicea's Chariot: The Warrior Queens.* London: Weidenfeld & Nicolson, 1988.

Hanawalt, Barbara A. *The Middle Ages: An Illustrated History.* New York: Oxford University Press, 1998.

Jones, Terry and Alan Ereira. *Crusades.* New York: Facts on File, 1995.

MacDonald, Allan John. *Hildebrand: A Life of Gregory VII.* Merrick, NY: Richwood Publishing Company, 1976.

Web Sites

Medieval Sourcebook: Empire and Papacy. [Online] Available http://www.fordham.edu/halsall/sbook1n.html (last accessed July 26, 2000).

"Patron Saints Index: Pope Gregory VII." *Catholic Forum.* [Online] Available http://www.catholic-forum.com/saints/saintg09.htm (last accessed July 26, 2000).

Henry the Navigator

Born 1394
Died 1460

Portuguese prince, supporter of exploration

As a supporter of some of the first European voyages of exploration, Prince Henry the Navigator of Portugal added immeasurably to Westerners' knowledge of other lands—yet he never actually took part in any voyages. Committed to spreading the Christian faith to other lands, he was very much a man of the Middle Ages, yet he helped bring about changes that would usher in the modern era.

A prophecy at his birth

Henry's father, John I, was the first king in the house of Aviz, which would rule Portugal for nearly two centuries beginning in 1385. A year later, Portugal signed a treaty with England, and to seal the agreement, Philippa of Lancaster, an English noblewoman, was married to King John. The couple had several sons, and the third one to survive—death in infancy or childhood was common in the Middle Ages—was Henry.

Medieval people placed great store by astrology, the belief that a person's fate is influenced by the position of the

"[The prince will] be engaged in important and propitious conquests in lands which were hidden from other men."

Horoscope prediction given at Henry's birth

Portrait: *Reproduced by permission of the Corbis Corporation.*

stars and planets at the time of their birth. Though there is no scientific basis for astrology, it is interesting to note that at his birth, Henry's astrological chart or horoscope predicted that the young prince would "be engaged in important and propitious [favorable] conquests in lands which were hidden from other men." It was a prophecy that would later come true.

Educated in Christian principles

Henry grew up with an education typical of a young prince, but because he had older brothers, he was not expected to rule. His mother was a devout Christian, and therefore he was taught on the one hand extensively from the Bible, in particular Christian principles of morality, or right and wrong. On the other hand, because kingdoms had to be defended through war, he received what was called "bodily training," or an education in how to fight and lead battles. Henry grew up to be tall, and though his complexion was naturally light, the time he spent outdoors gave him a tan. It was said that people who did know him thought he had a fierce expression, but in fact he was gentle by nature.

As a result of his education, young Henry had three strong aims in mind: to expand Portugal's commercial interests, to increase scientific knowledge, and to spread the Christian faith to other lands. Much of neighboring Spain remained in the hands of the rival Islamic or Muslim faith, as did North Africa across the Mediterranean Sea. Henry believed strongly in the spirit that had fueled the Crusades, wars of religious conquest to win lands from the Muslims and place them under the control of Christian Europe.

The crusade for Ceuta

In the summer of 1415, when Henry was twenty-one years old, his mother died, and on her deathbed, she gave each of her three sons a piece of what was believed to be the cross on which Jesus Christ was crucified. Though it is doubtful that anyone knew the location of the "true cross," medieval Europeans believed strongly in such relics, or objects with religious significance; and furthermore, Henry was deeply moved by the loss of his mother. This no doubt inspired him to undertake the first significant act of his adult life, a crusade to take Ceuta (THAY-ü-tah), a city in Morocco.

In August 1415, Henry helped lead the campaign for Ceuta, which turned out to be successful. This won him considerable honors, and put him a long way toward his life's mission, which was to learn more about the African continent and outlying islands. A year later, he sent the explorer Gonzalo Velho to the Canary Islands, off the northwest coast of Africa in the Atlantic Ocean. This was the beginning of his involvement in commercial quests to expand Portugal's empire.

Establishes "school" at Sagres

Perhaps to get away from his family and make a life for himself independent of their influence, in 1420 Henry moved to Lagos (LAH-gohs), on the southern coast of Portugal. He tried unsuccessfully to conquer the highly important city of Gibraltar (ji-BRAWL-tur), then controlled by the Moors, or Muslims from North Africa. Failing this, he turned his attention to gaining as much knowledge as he could about the "country" of Guinea (GI-nee).

Today there is a nation known as Guinea, but when Europeans of Henry's time used the term, they applied it broadly to the western coast of Africa. Henry had a lifelong interest in the region, and began gathering around him explorers and men of science who would help him gather knowledge about it. To this end, he established an informal "school" in the Portuguese city of Sagres (SAH-greesh), on the extreme southwestern tip of Portugal.

Successes and failures

The first major expedition launched by Henry's school took place from 1418 to 1420, and resulted in the establishment of Portugal's first overseas colony at Porto Santo on the Madeira (mah-DEER-uh) Islands to the northwest of the Canaries. Ships also began sailing south to explore the coast of Guinea, and as each expedition returned, Henry's cartographers (kar-TAHG-ruh-furz), or mapmakers, developed new maps incorporating the knowledge added by the returning explorers.

Cheng Ho

Like Henry the Navigator, Admiral Cheng Ho (jung-HOH; c. 1371–c. 1433) is a memorable figure in the history of exploration, but unlike Henry, Cheng actually led the voyages for which he is famous. Over the course of more than a quarter-century, he commanded a Chinese fleet that sailed to Southeast Asia, India, Persia, Arabia, and even Africa.

The son of Muslims in southern China, Cheng was born Ma Sanpao (MAH sahn-POW), and when he was twelve years old, he went to serve in the court of Prince Yan, the future emperor Yung-lo of China's Ming dynasty. When Yung-lo took power, he gave Ma Sanpao the new family name of Cheng, a sign of honor. At some point, Cheng was castrated and made a eunuch (YOO-nuk). When and why this happened is not known, though Chinese emperors often relied on eunuchs because they believed they could trust them around their many wives and concubines.

Initially the emperor put Cheng Ho to work building palaces in his capital city, but in 1405 he commissioned him as an admiral, a high-ranking naval officer equivalent to a general in the army. Yung-lo sent him on his first voyage, which lasted two years and involved some 27,000 men on more than sixty ships. They traveled to ports in Southeast Asia, as well as the islands of what is now western Indonesia, before reaching Ceylon and finally Calicut, in southern India.

Despite the fact that Henry's expeditions had the potential to add greatly to Portugal's wealth, he had many critics. Furthermore, he invested a great deal of his own money in the voyages, and for nearly fifteen years, his captains made little progress in finding a sea route to Guinea.

In September 1433, Henry's father died, and this forced him to turn his attention to family matters. His brother Edward I took the throne, but his reign was short and troubled, ending in his death in 1438. The new king, Afonso V, was Henry's nephew—but he was only five years old, and Henry had to assist in ruling the country as regent.

Later other counselors took over Henry's duties in the capital, and he was able to return to his primary interests. In 1437, he and his brother Ferdinand launched a campaign to

Though their purpose was peaceful, and they brought with them gifts for the princes they met, Yung-lo also intended for his fleet to demonstrate Chinese power in other lands. In any case, Cheng often became involved in conflicts, as on the first voyage, when a pirate attacked his fleet and killed some five thousand of his men. Cheng captured the pirate and brought him back in chains to China, where he was executed.

On a later voyage, the king of Ceylon (now Sri Lanka) tried to double-cross Cheng and attacked his ships while the Chinese were away in the Ceylonese capital. Learning of this, Cheng reasoned that the king had dispatched all his troops to the harbor and thus had left the city undefended, so he attacked the city. Victorious, he brought the king of Ceylon back to China, where he was treated with kindness, but was replaced with a ruler more favorable to Chinese interests.

Later voyages took Cheng and his fleet to Persia and Arabia, and even—on the fourth expedition (1413–15)—to Africa. The fleet returned from this voyage bringing with them a giraffe, which they presented to the emperor's court. After Yung-lo died in 1424, Cheng's future was uncertain, but finally in 1430, he and his fleet were allowed to embark on a seventh—and, as it turned out, last—voyage. They went as far as Hormuz in Persia, but Cheng himself died in Calicut. With him died a golden age of Chinese exploration, never to be repeated.

take the city of Tangier (tan-JEER) in Morocco. This turned out to be a massive failure, with the Moors capturing Ferdinand, who died in prison five years later.

A turning point

Devastated by the loss of Ferdinand and his failure in Tangier, Henry again concentrated on voyages along the African coast. He wanted to learn not just about the coastal regions, but about the interior, and encouraged his sea captains to use the continent's river systems as a means of reaching farther inland. Therefore he ordered the construction of an outpost at Arguin (ar-GWEEN) Island, off the coast of what is today the nation of Mauritania. This too led to a setback, as one of the captains he hired managed to steal part of the money Henry invested in the voyages.

Despite his many frustrations—and the fact that he was continuing to lose money—Henry was also starting to see some successes, particularly with his sailors' exploration of the Azores (uh-ZOHRZ), an island group west of Portugal. In 1454, the pope officially recognized the possessions gained by Henry's voyagers, and since all of Western Europe looked to the pope's spiritual leadership, this was an important victory. By the late 1440s and 1450s, Henry's interests had shifted from voyages for purely scientific purposes toward expeditions specifically intended to expand Portugal's commercial interests.

A Christian warrior to the end

One of those commercial interests was slavery, and in particular the traffic in human beings captured from Africa. Slavery had long before ceased to exist in Europe, but a new chapter in the history of the slave trade began in 1441, when one of Henry's captains presented him with fourteen slaves as a "gift." Many Portuguese favored the slave trade, which would grow in coming years, but Henry rejected it for both moral and practical reasons. On a practical level, he saw slavery as an unprofitable business, and on a moral level, he knew that it was not likely to produce many converts to Christianity.

During the 1450s, Henry's sailors continued to gather information about Africa while Henry himself became increasingly withdrawn from public contact. Yet he remained a crusader to the end, and his passions were stirred when in 1453 he learned that the Muslim Turks had conquered the Christian city of Constantinople (now Istanbul, Turkey), thus bringing an end to the Byzantine Empire. In 1458, the sixty-four-year-old Henry took part in a crusade, along with Afonso V, to take a town in Morocco held by the Muslims. Though the Portuguese were victorious in the battle, the tide of events was against them, and Morocco remained in the hands of the Muslims.

Henry knew he was dying, so he returned to Sagres in 1460 and made out his will. Unmarried, he had no children, and in any case, he left behind not a fortune but a considerable debt brought on by his years of investment without noticeable returns. Yet through his efforts, he opened up the world to European explorers, and helped launch the Age of Discovery that was just then beginning to dawn.

For More Information

Books

Fisher, Leonard Everett. *Prince Henry the Navigator*. New York: Macmillan, 1990.

Hale, John R. *Age of Exploration*. New York: Time-Life Books, 1974.

Levathes, Louise. *When China Ruled the Seas*. New York: Oxford University Press, 1996.

Simon, Charnan. *Henry the Navigator*. Chicago: Children's Press, 1993.

Web Sites

"Chinese Mariner Cheng Ho." [Online] Available http://www.china-page.org/chengho.html (last accessed July 26, 2000).

"Discoverers Web: Henry the Navigator." [Online] Available http://www.win.tue.nl/~engels/discovery/henry.html (last accessed July 26, 2000).

"European Voyages of Exploration: Prince Henry the Navigator." [Online] Available http://www.acs.ucalgary.ca/HIST/tutor/eurvoya/henry1.html (last accessed July 26, 2000).

"Henry the Navigator." [Online] Available http://www.thornr.demon.co.uk/kchrist/phenry.html (last accessed July 26, 2000).

Historians

The Venerable Bede

Born 672
Died 735

Anglo-Saxon historian
and theologian

Al-Mas'udi

Died 957

Arab historian

Ssu-ma Kuang

Born 1019
Died 1086

Chinese government
official and historian

Anna Comnena

Born c. 1083
Died 1148

Byzantine princess
and historian

The work of historians is always important, seldom more so than in the Middle Ages. Not only did people then lack modern forms of communication, but in Western Europe at least, the medieval period was a time when the pace of learning slowed for several centuries. Thus it became all the more important to access the wisdom of the past, a time when communication and learning had flourished under the civilizations of Greece and Rome. But history was also important as a means of guessing what might happen in the future. When the Anglo-Saxon historian St. Bede noted that the people of England had ceased to study the arts of war, he hinted that this might have disastrous consequences. Four centuries later, another English historian, William of Malmesbury (c. 1090–c. 1143), would describe the consequence of the English lack of preparedness when he chronicled the then-recent invasion led by **William the Conqueror** (see entry).

Bede, al-Mas'udi, Ssu-ma Kuang, and Anna Comnena came from a variety of places, as their names suggest: respectively, England, the Middle East, China, and Greece. Each had a different viewpoint on history, informed by differing life ex-

"As such peace and prosperity prevail these days, many ... have laid aside their weapons ... rather than study the arts of war. What the result of this will be, the future will show."

The Venerable Bede

periences. One was a priest, another a traveler, the third a government official, the last a princess—and as a woman, she had a particularly unique perspective. To varying degrees, each wrote history to serve their own purposes, yet each performed a service to the world by preserving a record of their time and place.

The Venerable Bede

Bede, often referred to as "The Venerable Bede," was born in England more than two centuries after Anglo-Saxon invaders from what is now Germany and Denmark swept in and conquered the Celtic peoples who had controlled Britain for nearly a millennium. To Bede, that invasion was a central event of his people's history, though later critics came to believe that he missed a larger perspective: in fact the invasion had been coming for a long time, and was not so much one event as a series of events.

The Venerable Bede.
Reproduced by permission of Archive Photos, Inc.

As was typical of intelligent young men in medieval Europe, Bede was trained for a career in the church. This began for him at the age of seven, when his parents put him in a monastery, a place where monks studied the Bible and the writings of early church fathers such as **Augustine** and **Gregory I** (see entries). His primary teacher was the abbot—that is, the head of the monastery—Ceolfrid (CHAYL-frid).

In 686, when Bede would have been about fourteen years old, the abbey was devastated with a plague, or an epidemic of disease, but he continued his studies. Despite the fact that he lived in England, far from the Italian and Greek centers of ancient European civilization, Bede became a master of the Latin and Greek languages, and even learned some Hebrew. He advanced rapidly in the church, becoming a deacon at age nineteen, even though that position was usually reserved for men much older. He was ordained as a priest at the age of thirty. Apart from a few short trips—most notably a visit to Lindisfarne, a celebrated English center of learning off the coast—Bede traveled little during his life.

Bede wrote numerous works on history and theology, or the analysis of religious faith. As a medieval scholar steeped in the teachings of the church, he saw history as an unfolding of God's purposes, and in his view, church history *was* history. Accordingly, his most famous work was *Historia ecclesiastica gentis Anglorum,* or *Ecclesiastical History of the English People* (731). The term "ecclesiastical" refers to the church, and Bede's historical writings in general make little mention of secular events, or things of a non-spiritual nature.

Despite the shortcomings in some of his historical analysis, most notably his reliance on questionable information concerning the distant past, Bede offered a valuable record of events in the early part of the medieval period. He died on May 25, 735, at the age of sixty-three, and within a century, the term "Venerable," meaning distinguished, was attached to his name. In 1899 he was canonized, or recognized as a saint.

Page from a late eighth-century transcription of the Venerable Bede's most famous work, *Historia ecclesiastica gentis Anglorum.* *Reproduced by permission of the Pierpont Morgan Library.*

Al-Mas'udi

The writings of al-Mas'udi (mahs-oo-DEE) illustrate the heights that Arab and Islamic civilization reached in the Middle East during the medieval period. His engaging style and talent for insightful observation, along with his comprehensive approach to the history of his people, earned him great acclaim. Later generations in Europe would dub al-Mas'udi the "Herodotus of the Arabs," a reference to the first true historian, Herodotus (hur-AHD-uh-tus; c. 484–c. 424 B.C.) of ancient Greece.

Born in Baghdad, now the capital of Iraq, al-Mas'udi descended from a close friend of the prophet **Muhammad** (see entry). He apparently traveled widely during his life, though the extent of his travels is not clear, and it appears that he never actually visited Ceylon (modern Sri Lanka) or the China Sea, as he claimed. Yet in the period from 915 to 917 he traveled eastward to Persia and India, then voyaged to Zanzibar on the east coast of Africa and Oman on the Arabian Peninsula. He made a number of other journeys, to Palestine, the Caspian Sea, and other areas, over the decade that followed. As to the purpose of al-Mas'udi's journeys, this is not known. Perhaps like Herodotus centuries before, he was collecting information for his historical writings; in any case, his travels certainly informed his writing, which shows an impressive range of knowledge.

Of the more than thirty writings attributed to al-Mas'udi, only two can be clearly identified as his. The more famous of these has been translated as *The Meadows of Gold,* and consists of two volumes that respectively recount the history of the world prior to and after the time when Muhammad brought the Islamic message. His work has provided historians with valuable insights on the life of Arab leaders such as Harun al-Rashid (see box in El Cid entry) and others. Al-Mas'udi spent his later years in Cairo, Egypt, where he died in 957.

Ssu-ma Kuang

Unlike most historians, Ssu-ma Kuang (sü-MAH GWAHNG) participated not only in the writing of history, but also—in his capacity as a government official in China's Sung dynasty—in the making of history. In fact, it was his high position in the court that led the Sung emperor to commission him to write a history of China, known in English as the *Comprehensive Mirror for Aid in Government.*

A talented young man, Ssu-ma Kuang completed his education at age nineteen and, as was the custom in China, took an examination to enter the civil service, or government bureaucracy. He rose quickly through the ranks, and legend has it that he made a name for himself when he saved a drowning child by breaking the water tank into which the child had fallen.

When it came to changes in the government and life of China, however, Ssu-ma Kuang favored a more deliberate approach than the one he had used to save the drowning child. He was committed to the principles of Confucius (c. 551–479 B.C.), a highly influential ancient Chinese philosopher who taught respect for elders and people in positions of authority. Like Confucius, Ssu-ma Kuang was a conservative, or someone who favors slow change. This put him at odds with Wang An-shih (1021–1086), another prominent government official who favored sweeping reforms to the Sung government.

Ssu-ma Kuang's work as a historian began some time before 1064, when he presented the emperor with a chronological table, or timeline, of Chinese history from its beginnings to the present day. The emperor was so impressed with this and later work that he ordered Ssu-ma Kuang to prepare a full-scale history of China, which would become the *Comprehensive Mirror.* At about the same time he received this directive, however, Ssu-ma Kuang clashed with Wang An-shih, and was forced to leave the court. During the years that followed, he devoted himself to the writing of his history.

The *Comprehensive Mirror* is not the most exciting work ever written, but it is certainly thorough. Ssu-ma Kuang and the scholars working with him carefully checked a range of historical documents, and were painstaking in their efforts to achieve accuracy. Finally, in 1084, he presented it to the emperor, who gave it his approval. So, too, have many later historians, who have seen the book as a significant milestone in the development of history as an area of study. In part from Ssu-ma Kuang's writing, the Chinese developed a view of history not as a straight-line progression, but as a series of cycles, with the rise and fall of each successive dynasty merely a part of the cyclical process.

In his later years, Ssu-ma Kuang became increasingly involved in power struggles with Wang An-shih, and by 1085 he had returned to a position of influence. He was able to defeat many of Wang's reforms by 1086, the year in which both men died. So great was Ssu-ma Kuang's position of honor in the government that all business in the Chinese capital ceased on the day of his funeral. But his victory over Wang was not complete: subsequent years saw a continued battle in the Chinese leadership between those who adhered to Ssu-ma Kuang's conservatism and those who favored Wang An-shih's reformist approach.

Anna Comnena

Not only was she the world's first notable female historian, Anna Comnena (kahm-NEE-nuh) had a remarkable front-row seat for one of the most monumental events in history. It so happened that she was the eldest daughter of the Byzantine emperor Alexis I Comnenus, who in 1095 requested help from the pope in fighting the Turks, who were threatening his land from the east. The result was the First Crusade (1095–99), in which the Western Europeans marched through the Byzantine Empire on their way to seize Palestine from the Muslims. About twelve years old at the time, Anna saw these events unfold, and recounted them in her *Alexiad,* a record of her father's reign.

Anna was born in the Byzantine capital of Constantinople (now Istanbul, Turkey), which at that time was Europe's leading center of culture. As a princess, she received a highly advanced education, and like many Greeks of her time, she came to regard Western Europeans as uncouth barbarians compared to the highly civilized people of the Byzantine Empire. Her later experience with the crusaders would reinforce this opinion.

In 1097, when she was fourteen, Anna married Nicephorus Bryennius (ny-SEF-ur-us bry-EN-ee-us), a historian eighteen years her senior. Despite the fact that the empire had once been ruled by a woman, **Irene of Athens** (see entry), Anna had no plans to take the throne, especially because she had a younger brother, John. Yet at the age of thirty-five, she launched an unsuccessful plot to make her husband emperor. John found out about the conspiracy, and sent Anna away to a monastery for the rest of her life. There she wrote the *Alexiad,* a history of the period from 1069 to 1118—that is, from the time her uncle Isaac Comnenus established the dynasty to the end of her father's reign.

The suffix *-ad* in Greek usually means that a work is the glorious tale of a great nation, and certainly Anna's history provides an image of the Byzantine Empire under her family's rule as a highly civilized realm. In her writings on the behavior of the crusaders from Western Europe, she portrayed them as greedy invaders who, while pretending to help her father, were actually interested in taking advantage of him. Though there is no question Anna had a prejudiced view toward Western Europeans in general, and the crusaders in particular, her assessment was largely accurate, as subsequent events illustrated. The crusaders did little to help the Byzantines, and in 1204 they actually turned against their supposed ally, seizing control of Constantinople and holding it for fifty-seven years.

For More Information

Books

Barrett, Tracy. *Anna of Byzantium*. New York: Delacorte Press, 1999.

Encyclopedia of World Biography, second edition. Detroit: Gale, 1998.

Hill, Frank Ernest. *Famous Historians*. New York: Dodd, Mead, 1966.

Web Sites

"Bede the Venerable, Priest, Monk, Scholar." [Online] Available http://justus.anglican.org/resources/bio/169.html (last accessed July 26, 2000).

"Female Hero: Anna Comnena." *Women in World History*. [Online] Available http://www.womeninworldhistory.com/heroine5.html (last accessed July 26, 2000).

"Medieval Sourcebook: Abul Hasan Ali Al-Masu'di (Masoudi) (c. 895?–957 CE) The Book of Golden Meadows, c. 940 CE."

Medieval Sourcebook. [Online] Available http://www.fordham.edu/halsall/source/masoudi.html (last accessed July 26, 2000).

"Medieval Sourcebook: Anna Comnena: *The Alexiad:* On the Crusades." *Medieval Sourcebook*. [Online] Available http://www.fordham.edu/halsall/source/comnena-cde.html (last accessed July 26, 2000).

"The Venerable Bede." [Online] Available http://www.cohums.ohio-state.edu/history/people/crisp.23/bede.htm (last accessed July 26, 2000).

Holy Roman Emperors

Otto the Great

Born 912
Died 973

German king,
Holy Roman emperor

Otto III

Born 980
Died 1002

German king,
Holy Roman emperor

Frederick I Barbarossa

Born 1123
Died 1190

German king,
Holy Roman emperor

Frederick II

Born 1194
Died 1250

Sicilian and German king,
Holy Roman emperor

There is a joke almost as old as the Middle Ages themselves, to the effect that the Holy Roman Empire was neither holy, nor Roman, nor an empire. Actually the observation, originally made by the French writer Voltaire in the 1700s, has a grain of truth. A revival of the realm established first under **Charlemagne** (see entry), the Holy Roman Empire represented an attempt to restore the glories of the Roman Empire of old, but its center was in Germany, and it was seldom unified. As for being "holy," this title referred only to the fact that rulers of the empire, like the four men profiled here, were traditionally crowned by the pope. Ironically, as the career of Emperor **Henry IV** (see dual entry with Gregory VII) illustrated, the popes were to be the emperors' greatest foes in their quest for power.

"The Renewal of the Roman Empire"

Inscription on seal ring of Otto III, signifying his life's goal

From Charlemagne to Otto

By the time Pope Leo III crowned him "Emperor of the Romans" in 800, Charlemagne controlled most of Western Europe. Initially it seemed that he had revived the Western Roman Empire, but a number of forces conspired to prevent this from happening. One was the resistance of the Eastern Roman Empire, which still existed—and would continue to exist until 1453—in the form of Byzantium. Another was the fact that Charlemagne's successors were not his equals. Finally, Charlemagne's son ended all imperial hopes by dividing his lands between his three heirs. In 911, the year before the future Otto the Great was born, the last of Charlemagne's line lost his throne.

Germany at that time was mostly covered with forests, and geography—mountains, rivers, and other natural barriers—served to further divide the land. The region consisted of five duchies, or realms controlled by a duke: Franconia, Saxony, Thuringia (thoor-INJ-ee-uh), Swabia (SWAY-bee-uh), and Bavaria. The dukes elected one of their members as king, and Otto's father, Henry the Fowler of Saxony (c. 876–936), was elected king in 919. Despite the election, however, he had to fight to bring the other duchies under his control.

Otto the Great's early years

Otto spent his early years training for leadership, which for a medieval king involved a great deal of education in fighting, but little in the way of classroom education. Though he would later support learning in his kingdom, Otto himself only learned to read and write in his middle age. At the age of eighteen, he was married to Edith, an Anglo-Saxon princess from England with whom he had two sons. Six years later, Otto's father died, and he was elected king of Germany.

From the beginning, Otto faced opposition from all sides, including a number of revolts instigated by a brother and a half-brother. By 939, however, he had resolved these problems—at least for the time being—and the kingdom enjoyed relative peace for the next twelve years. During this time, he consolidated his power by placing trustworthy family members in positions of influence, and led a successful campaign to subdue Bohemia in 950.

Otto is crowned Holy Roman emperor

Edith died in 946, but Otto would marry a second time. Unlike his father, Otto had dreams larger than Germany itself, and made it his goal to restore the empire of Charlemagne by conquering Italy. An opportunity presented itself in 950, when a princess named Adelaide, widow of the king of Italy, sent a plea for help. She had been imprisoned by a noble named Berengar (BAYR-un-gur), who had seized the throne, and Otto marched his troops into Italy, rescued the princess, and married her.

In the years immediately following, a number of problems—including a revolt at home, led by one of his sons—prevented Otto from completing his Italian campaign. He also faced an enemy that had long plagued Germany's eastern borders: the Magyars, who would later establish the nation of Hungary. In a battle on August 10, 955, Otto decisively defeated them, in the process earning the title "Otto the Great." Later that year, Adelaide gave birth to a son, who would reign as Otto II from 973 to 983.

Otto the Great.

In 961, Otto and Adelaide led a sizeable army into Italy, and on February 2, 962, Pope John XII crowned the couple as emperor and empress. Otto would spend most of his remaining years in Italy, fighting to maintain control. In 972, he arranged the marriage of his son to the Byzantine princess Theophano (thee-AHF-uh-noh), a move designed to ensure his family's future imperial status. Later that year, he returned to his beloved Germany, where he died on May 7, 973.

From Otto the Great to Otto III

Otto III, born seven years after the death of his grandfather, would grow up nourished on dreams of empire. In large part, this was due to the influence of Adelaide and Theophano, who raised him on tales of Byzantine glory. Indeed, the role of women was a consistent and powerful theme in the story of the medieval Holy Roman emperors, who were strongly impacted by their mothers and wives. After the death of Otto II in 983, Theophano and Adelaide ruled the empire as regents until Otto came of age at fourteen.

Like his grandfather, Otto spent much of his career in Rome, where in 996 his cousin Pope Gregory V crowned him emperor. Two years later, Gregory died, and Otto made his friend Gerbert pope as Sylvester II. Otto the Great had established the tradition of Holy Roman emperors choosing popes when, a year after his coronation, he had removed the corrupt John XII from his papal seat. In so doing, the grandfather had established a source of later conflict with the popes.

The fact that Otto III spent most of his reign in Rome rather than in Germany indicates his grand designs of a restored Roman Empire. So, too, does the motto on his seal ring, which he used to inscribe official documents: "The Renewal of the Roman Empire." He sent a crown to the Byzantine emperor **Basil II** (see entry), proclaiming him ruler of the East as Otto was ruler of the West. Basil had no interest in forming such an alliance, but he did offer his niece in marriage to Otto. Twenty-two-year-old Otto, however, did not live long enough to marry.

From Otto III to Frederick I

Power in the Holy Roman Empire passed from Otto's Saxon house to the Salian (SAY-lee-un) house, which would include Henry IV, in 1024. The Salian line ended when Henry V died without an heir, and was replaced in 1138 by the Hohenstaufen (hoh-un-SHTOW-fin) dynasty. The Hohenstaufens would maintain the throne until 1250, and their line would include Frederick I and II.

Frederick I, nicknamed Barbarossa (bar-buh-ROH-suh) or "Red Beard," was born more than a century after Otto III. A nephew of Hohenstaufen founder Conrad III, he joined his uncle on the disastrous Second Crusade in 1147, and learned much from the mistakes made by the Europeans in that doomed effort. Conrad died in 1152 without an heir, but he had designated nineteen-year-old Frederick as his successor.

Frederick I fights to control Italy

Like his predecessors, Frederick would spend much of his career trying to maintain control over Italy. This enduring instability, in fact, would ensure that the "Holy Roman Empire" remained little more than a name. Crowned emperor in 1155 (though he had actually assumed power three years earlier), he established Europe's first university in the Italian city of Bologna (buh-LOHN-yuh) in 1158. In 1154, however, he had become drawn into a long and essentially fruitless campaign to subdue Lombardy, a large region in northern Italy.

In this effort, Frederick encountered a number of foes. One was Pope Alexander III (ruled 1159–81), who in 1160 excommunicated Frederick, or formally expelled him from the church. In 1167, Alexander helped organize the Lombard League, an alliance of cities opposed to Frederick. Then in 1175 Frederick began to have trouble with Henry the Lion, Duke of Saxony, who opposed him both in Germany and Italy.

Frederick defeated Henry's forces in Germany in 1181, and in 1183 signed the Peace of Constance, which gave Lombard League cities their freedom. He strengthened his position in Italy by arranging the marriage of his son, the future Henry VI, to the Norman princess Constance, who controlled Sicily and the southern portion of the Italian Peninsula.

Frederick I Barbarossa.
Reproduced by permission of the Library of Congress.

The death of Frederick I

He also restored his relationship with the popes, and in 1189 Pope Clement III convinced him to join **Richard I** (see entry) and Philip of France in the Third Crusade. Like many crusaders before, Frederick became embroiled in conflicts with the Byzantine Empire, and he never made it to the intended destination of Palestine. Having defeated Byzantine forces in battle, he and his armies were crossing a river in Anatolia (modern-day Turkey) when Frederick drowned in late 1189.

During his reign, Frederick strengthened the feudal system in Germany, and would be remembered as one of his nation's greatest heroes. According to a German legend, Frederick was not dead but asleep at a stone table in Thuringia, his red beard continuing to grow—and when Germany needed him again, he would awaken. Eventually the myth would also become associated with his grandson, Frederick II.

The early career of Frederick II

It was ironic that Frederick II would be associated with a Germanic legend since he was not completely German, and only spent time in Germany because his role required it. Raised in Sicily by his mother Constance, Frederick at age fifteen married another Constance, sister of Pedro II of Aragon in Spain. Despite the fact that this was an arranged marriage—like most unions involving royal figures of the Middle Ages—it appears that Frederick and Constance grew to genuinely love one another. When she died in 1122, he had his crown placed in her tomb.

Frederick was extremely well educated for a medieval ruler, and would maintain a lifelong interest in the arts and sciences. Affairs of state plagued his early years, however, and since he was something of a foreigner, he had to spend much of his time securing his power in Germany. Soon after he was crowned German king in 1215, he made a promise to undertake a crusade; however, he would spend the next fourteen years putting off the intended trip.

The Sixth Crusade

German kings usually became Holy Roman emperors, but not always, and Frederick had to wait until 1220 to receive the imperial crown. Widowed two years later, he married Isabella, sister of King Henry III of England, in 1225. He faced continual pressure from the popes to go on his promised crusade, and in the late 1220s Gregory IX excommunicated him for his failure to do so. This seemed to appeal to Frederick's cantankerous nature, and he responded by going to the Holy Land anyway.

The result was the Sixth Crusade (1228–29), which was chiefly a matter of negotiation rather than warfare. By then, Europe had lost much of its crusading spirit, and the shrewd Frederick—who, unlike most Europeans, had a profound respect for the Muslims and their culture—secured a treaty that briefly restored Christian control of Jerusalem.

The court of Frederick II

The real fighting was back in Europe, where the pope and other enemies threatened his control over Sicily and other lands. These efforts occupied most of Frederick's attention during the last two decades of his life, but he found time to establish a highly organized state in Sicily. He also gathered around him so many scholars and artists that his court had no rival for cultural achievements.

Frederick distinguished himself by his willingness to associate not only with Christians, but with Muslims and Jews, and he drew representatives of all these cultures to Sicily. He even wrote a scholarly work, *On the Art of Hunting with Hawks,* and encouraged the arts of painting, sculpture, and architecture in Sicily.

Though he became the source of many bizarre rumors—for instance, many referred to Frederick, notorious for his opposition to the popes, as "The Antichrist"—he was undoubtedly one of the most fascinating men of his time. He died on December 13, 1250, at the age of fifty-six. On his tomb were inscribed the words, "If probity [high ideals], reason, abundance of virtue, nobility of birth, could forfend [prevent] death, Frederick, who is here entombed, would not be dead."

Frederick II. *Reproduced by permission of Archive Photos, Inc.*

For More Information

Books

Barraclough, Geoffrey. *The Origins of Modern Germany.* New York: Norton, 1984.

Berry, Erick and Herbert Best. *Men Who Changed the Map, A.D. 400 to 1914.* New York: Funk & Wagnalls, 1968.

Duckett, Eleanor. *Death and Life in the Tenth Century.* Ann Arbor: University of Michigan Press, 1971.

Encyclopedia of World Biography, second edition. Detroit: Gale, 1998.

Munz, Peter. *Frederick Barbarossa: A Study in Medieval Politics.* Ithaca, NY: Cornell University Press, 1969.

Web Sites

"Chronology of Germany." [Online] Available http://www.ac.wwu.edu/~stephan/Rulers/chron.germany.html (last accessed July 26, 2000).

"Die Deutschekulturseite—Otto I" (in English). [Online] Available http://res3.geocities.com/Athens/Olympus/5011/otto.html (last accessed July 26, 2000).

Innocent III

Born c. 1161
Died 1216

Italian pope

The papacy, or office of the pope, reached its peak during the reign of Innocent III, who held the position from 1198 to 1216. A ruthless negotiator and an expert manipulator of men, he was a politician who outwitted some of the greatest strategic minds on the European continent. Yet it would be a mistake to view him merely as power-hungry or politically ambitious; Innocent was also a man of sincere religious beliefs whose passion for what he believed was right actually contributed to some of the worst excesses of his rule.

The church had come a long way since St. Benedict (see box) led his monks to new standards of discipline more than six centuries before. Nor was the pope's role under the same threats faced by Urban II (see box) a century before Innocent. Urban had declared war on religious enemies overseas; Innocent's launch of the Albigensian Crusade proved that the church could deal even more severely with perceived enemies at home.

"So the great Pope passed and with him, in some sense, passed the greatness of the medieval Papacy itself, for none was to arise after Innocent who was to be, as he had been, the arbiter [controller] of the destinies of Europe."

L. Elliott Binns, Innocent III

Portrait: *Reproduced by permission of the Corbis Corporation.*

Benedict of Nursia

Innocent represented the church at the height of its wealth and earthly power, whereas St. Benedict of Nursia (c. 480–547) symbolized an entirely different side of the church. Benedict's focus was exactly the opposite of Innocent's, and if he had been offered wealth and power, he would likely have shunned it. Though there had been monks before Benedict, it was his achievement to give order and discipline to the monastic movement.

According to his biographer, Pope **Gregory I** (see entry), Benedict was a serious young man from the beginning, and as a teenager shied away from the wickedness he saw in Rome. He resolved to live a life of solitude in a cave, where a kindly old monk helped him by bringing him bread and water every day. Nonetheless, Gregory as-sured his readers, Satan came many times to tempt Benedict, at one point assuming the form of a beautiful young woman. Benedict mastered his lust by flinging himself into a patch of briars and thorns.

After he had spent three years as a hermit, Benedict was approached by a group of monks who wanted him to teach them discipline. Benedict agreed to be their master, but warned them that he would be a stern leader. They must not have believed him, because they accepted his leadership and then became so disillusioned with his severity that they tried to poison him. Disgusted, Benedict went back to his cave.

Eventually, however, so many followers gathered around him that Benedict decided he would have to establish a monastery. He chose Monte Cassino, for-

A pope before he was a priest

It would be ironic indeed if this most un-innocent of men had been given that name at birth, but in fact he was born Lothario de Segni (SAYN-yee). Like many another pope, he came from an Italian noble family and received the finest education available at what were then Europe's two greatest universities, in Paris and Bologna (buh-LOHN-yuh), Italy.

It was one of the many curious facts of Innocent's career that he had not even been ordained, or formally appointed, as a priest when he became pope at age thirty-seven. He had reached the position of deacon, an office in the church below that of priest, when he was twenty-seven. Three years later, thanks in large part to a good relationship he had culti-

St. Benedict of Nursia (center). *Reproduced by permission of Archive Photos, Inc.*

tablished a convent, a place for nuns, at Monte Cassino.

Benedict died in 547, but the Benedictine Rule—that is, the system of life he had established for his monastery—long outlasted him. During his time, monks had tended to apply a variety of systems, some even more severe than Benedict's. Benedict discouraged his followers from going to the kind of extraordinary measures taken by lone figures such as Simeon Stylites (see box in Augustine entry). Other monastic systems emphasized the relationship between the monks and their leader, whereas Benedict's placed its emphasis on the relationship between monks. As pope, Gregory I heartily approved of the Benedictine Rule; and by the 800s, it became the prevailing monastic system in Western Europe.

merly the site of a temple honoring the god Apollo. Later his sister Scholastica es-

vated with Pope Clement III (ruled 1187–91), he was promoted to cardinal, the highest position short of pope.

Cardinals took part in the elections of popes, and Lothario's colleagues voted him to the church's highest position upon the death of Celestine III in 1198. He then chose the name of Innocent, and six weeks after his election was hastily ordained as a priest.

Ruler of kings

Innocent was the first pope to refer to his office as the "Vicar of Christ"—a title, meaning that the pope was Christ's direct representative on Earth, that all subsequent popes have

Urban II

Urban II, most noted for starting the First Crusade in 1095, assumed the position of pope a few years after **Gregory VII**. While Gregory had been perhaps the most important pope of the Middle Ages, his troubles with Emperor **Henry IV** (see dual entry with Gregory VII)—troubles Urban inherited—had left Rome a heap of smoking rubble. Therefore Urban wisely chose to stay away from the city, home of the papacy, and spend much of his time as pope traveling through Catholic realms.

Gregory had come from poverty, but Urban, born Odo in France, came from nobility. Perhaps his noble upbringing, and the fact that he had not had to fight for everything in life, taught him to be a bit more accommodating toward rivals: unlike Gregory, he knew when to give in, and often made concessions to powerful French leaders.

Urban was the first pope to model the papal government on that of a European monarchy; thenceforth, and up to the present day, the center of papal power would resemble a royal court in function. Heavily influenced by the monastic system at Cluny, where as a young man he had developed a passion for reform, he set about changing the church's finances. Also, like popes before and since, he became heavily involved with European political affairs.

He arranged a marriage between two supporters, Matilda of Tuscany (see box in Gregory VII and Henry IV entry) and Count Welf of Bavaria; and though the mar-

used. It was just one of the many extravagant claims Innocent made for the papacy.

Innocent believed that the popes, "seated on the throne of dignity ... judge in justice even the kings themselves." He participated in a seemingly endless series of intrigues with political leaders of Europe, promoting the career of **Frederick II** (see Holy Roman Emperors entry) as Holy Roman emperor and tangling with King John of England (see box in Eleanor of Aquitaine entry).

Angered by John's refusal to pay him what he considered his fair share of England's finances, Innocent placed England under what was called the interdict in 1208. For six years, until John relented, all religious services in the country were forbidden. Later Innocent did the same thing to the riage ended badly when Welf learned that Matilda intended to leave her inheritance to the church and not to him, Urban was able to use both of them against his archenemy, Henry IV. In contrast to Henry, there were a number of European leaders who accepted Urban's leadership unquestioningly: not only Matilda, but Henry's son Conrad, a number of Norman rulers, and the kings of Spain.

The latter were engaged in a war to take their land from the Muslims, a war from which **El Cid** (see entry) was to emerge the most noted hero. Perhaps it was from this conflict that Urban first hatched the idea of the Crusades. Whatever the case, when Byzantium's Alexis I Comnenus—father of **Anna Comnena** (see Historians entry)—sent him a request for a few troops to help battle the Turks, Urban began to conceive of a vast "holy war" to seize Palestine from Muslim hands.

Urban announced the idea at the Council of Clermont in France in 1095, where he made a stirring and memorable speech. This would ultimately lead to some two centuries of fighting, but none of the Crusades was destined to be as successful (from the viewpoint of the Europeans, that is) as the first. It ended in 1098 with the capture of Jerusalem and three other "crusader states" in what is now Israel, Lebanon, and Syria.

Ironically, Urban died two weeks before Jerusalem's capture. He had lived to see his old foe Henry punished, however, by being denied participation in the crusade.

powerful King Philip II Augustus of France. Thus he proved that although he did not command armies as large as those of Europe's monarchs, he still ruled their people's hearts and minds, and could undermine a king whenever he chose.

Reforms of church law

Having been a student of law at the University of Bologna, Innocent set out to reform the laws of the church. Those laws, he maintained, should govern the actions of church leaders throughout Christendom, and secular laws should hold secondary importance. Within the church, he undertook a campaign against simony, or the buying and selling of church offices, and reintroduced discipline to monasteries that had become too relaxed in recent years.

One of the most important aspects of Innocent's role as lawgiver was his convening of the Fourth Lateran Council in Rome in 1215. Among the many concepts established at this highly important meeting of more than a thousand church officials was the idea that Catholics should go to confession at least once a year. Formerly church members had believed that they should make confession—that is, tell a priest about their sins—just once in a lifetime; within three centuries of Innocent's time, confession was a once-a-week event.

Two uncontrollable crusades

By the time of Innocent's rule, Europeans had engaged in a century of crusades intended to take control of the Holy Land from Muslims. Except for the First Crusade, they were a disaster, and perhaps none were worse than the two that occurred under Innocent's leadership: the Fourth Crusade (1202–4) and the Children's Crusade. The latter was an absolutely miserable affair, whose participants mostly ended up captured and sold as slaves; and the former ended with the takeover of Constantinople and part of the Byzantine Empire by greedy knights representing business interests in Venice.

Actually, the two crusades were not really Innocent's fault. Though he can be blamed for starting the Fourth Crusade, he intended for it to result in the capture of Jerusalem, not Christian Constantinople, and he heartily disapproved of the so-called crusaders' actions. The fact that the Fourth Crusade went as it did, and that the Children's Crusade even occurred, illustrated the limits even of Innocent's power.

The attack on the Cathars

There were other crusades, however, over which Innocent seemed to be perfectly in control. Most notable was the Albigensian Crusade (al-buh-JIN-see-un; 1208–29), an attack on the Cathars, a sect in southern France that taught that the physical world was evil. Because God had also created the physical world, the church judged this belief heretical, or something that went against established teachings.

The Albigensian Crusade would later lead to the Inquisition, a wholesale attempt to root out heresy under Pope Gregory IX in 1231. A positive side effect of the crusade, however, was the introduction of mendicant groups of friars—preachers and teachers who survived by begging alms—under **St. Francis of Assisi** and St. Dominic (see St. Francis of Assisi entry and box). The Franciscans reached out with compassion to the poor, and the Dominicans tried to reason with unbelievers. Both represented the gentler side of the church, quite unlike the murder and mayhem sweeping southern France as part of Innocent's crusade.

Most powerful man in Europe

Another outgrowth of the Albigensian Crusade, a "holy war" that outlasted Innocent by many years, was the strengthening of the French royal house. By seizing lands belonging to noblemen in southern France, the church aided the kings of France, who would in turn try to assert their power over the popes. This led to a clash between King Philip IV and Pope Boniface VIII (see box in Gregory I entry), a conflict Boniface was destined to lose. Six years later, the French king would move the papal seat from Rome to the city of Avignon in southern France.

That conflict, however, still lay far in the future when Innocent died of malaria in May 1216. As he breathed his last, the papacy was secure in its absolute power over all of Western Europe. Yet, almost as a sign of things to come, robbers broke into the place where Innocent's body was prepared for burial, and on the night before the funeral stripped him of his clothes and jewels. The next day the corpse was found, half-naked, and the man who had briefly held the most powerful position in Europe was laid to rest.

For More Information

Books

Binns, L. Elliott. *Innocent III*. London: Methuen, 1968.

McDonald, Father Stephen James. *Bible History with a History of the Church*. New York: Row, Peterson and Company, 1940.

Rice, Edward. *A Young People's Pictorial History of the Church.* Text adapted by Blanche Jennings Thompson. New York: Farrar, Straus, 1963.

Web Sites

"The Abbey of Montecassino: Life of St. Benedict." [Online] Available http://www.officine.it/montecassino/storia_e/benedett.htm (last accessed July 26, 2000).

Brusher, the Rev. Joseph, S. J. "Popes through the Ages." [Online] Available http://www.ewtn.com/library/CHRIST/POPES.TXT (last accessed July 26, 2000).

"Catholic Encyclopedia: List of Popes." *Catholic Encyclopedia.* [Online] Available http://www.newadvent.org/cathen/12272b.htm (last accessed July 26, 2000).

"Chronology of Popes." *Information Please.* [Online] Available http://looksmart.infoplease.com/ce5/CE039386.html (last accessed July 26, 2000).

"The 11th to the 13th Centuries: Innocent III and the Great Schism." [Online] Available http://www.mcauley.acu.edu.au/~yuri/ecc/mod5.html (last accessed July 26, 2000).

"Saint Benedict of Nursia." *Order of Saint Benedict.* [Online] Available http://www.osb.org/gen/bendct.html (last accessed July 26, 2000).

Irene of Athens

Born c. 752
Died 803

Byzantine empress

Irene of Athens was the only woman to serve as sole ruler over the Byzantine Empire, and by calling the Seventh Ecumenical Council, she helped bring an end to the iconoclastic controversy that had rocked Byzantine society for years. Ironically, however, her greatest impact on history was unexpected. The Byzantine emperor controlled what remained of the Roman Empire, but according to Roman law, no woman could legally rule. Therefore when Irene took control it could be claimed that the Roman throne was vacant, and this gave the pope the opportunity to recognize **Charlemagne** (see entry) as the ruler of a new Roman Empire.

The iconoclastic controversy

The Byzantine Empire, or Byzantium (bi-ZAN-tee-um), grew out of the Eastern Roman Empire. After the collapse of the Roman Empire's western portion in 476, the two former halves of the empire grew apart. Eventually the Greek Orthodox (Eastern) and Roman Catholic (Western) churches would part ways, and one of the central issues that brought about this division was the iconoclastic (eye-kahn-oh-KLAS-tik) controversy.

Byzantine emperor Leo III (ruled 717–41) declared that all icons, or images of religious figures, were idols. An idol is a statue of a god, and the Bible had forbidden idol worship; therefore Leo and his followers, who called themselves iconoclasts, began destroying all religious images. Under Constantine V (ruled 741–75) the division between iconoclasts and iconophiles (eye-KAHN-oh-fylz), or people who believed that there was nothing sinful about worshiping religious images, became even more severe. This led to acts of violence as iconoclasts destroyed images, often killing the priests who tried to protect their churches.

Irene takes power

The future empress Irene came from an old family of Athens, the center of Greek culture. She was said to be a woman of great beauty, and thus she won the admiration of Leo IV, son of Constantine V. The two married in 769, when Irene was seventeen years old, and a year later, they had a son, Constantine VI.

Leo died in 780, and many claimed that Irene poisoned him in order to take power herself. However, she could never legally rule the empire: the emperor held a number of offices, including that of commander-in-chief of the military, which were simply off-limits to women. Furthermore, under Roman law succession was not hereditary: in other words, an emperor could not simply pass his throne on to his son, let alone his wife or daughter, because his replacement had to be elected by the leaders of the government. Those leaders chose ten-year-old Constantine VI as the new emperor, but Irene promptly took power as regent, someone who governs a country when the monarch is unable to do so.

Long a supporter of the iconophiles, Irene now began slowly restoring icon-worship. In the Greek Orthodox Church, the patriarch (PAYT-ree-ark) of Constantinople held a position similar to that of the pope, leader of the Roman Catholic Church; and when the iconoclast Paul IV died in 784, she replaced him with a patriarch sympathetic to the iconophile cause. She began removing generals and other officials loyal to the iconoclasts, and by 786 was prepared to make an even bolder step.

The Seventh Ecumenical Council

Many of the beliefs accepted by most Christians today were established not by the Bible, but by ecumenical (ek-yoo-MIN-i-kul; across all faiths) councils. The First Ecumenical Council had met in the city of Nicaea (nie-SEE-uh) in Asia Minor, modern-day Turkey, in 325; now Irene convened the Seventh Ecumenical Council to address the issue of icon-worship.

On May 31, 786, a group of religious leaders, including representatives sent by the pope, tried to meet in Constantinople, the Byzantine capital. By then, however, sixteen-year-old Constantine VI had begun to rebel against his mother, and troops loyal to him broke up the meeting.

Irene responded by sending the soldiers to Asia, where she claimed they were needed to defend the empire, and replaced them with a unit more favorable to her position. Having thus cleared the way, Irene arranged for the gathering to be held at Nicaea. Though she did not join the group of more than three hundred bishops who met between September 13 and October 13, 787, Irene managed the proceedings from Constantinople. As expected, the council restored the worship of icons.

Conflict with her son

Eager to establish her position, in 782 Irene had tried to arrange the marriage of her son to the daughter of Charlemagne, the most powerful ruler in Western Europe other than the pope. Charlemagne called off the marriage in 786, probably as a response to the fact that she had planned to convene the ecumenical council without consulting him first. Therefore in 788, she married Constantine to the daughter of a wealthy official in Greece.

Up to this point, Irene had maintained the pretense that Constantine was the real power in Byzantium, but when

Yang Kuei-fei

Like Irene, Yang Kuei-fei (YAHNG gway-FAY; d. 756) exerted enormous influence over a great empire; but unlike Irene, she did so from the background, and never officially ruled. Yang Kuei-fei was a concubine—a woman whose role toward her husband is like that of a wife, but without the social and legal status of a wife—to Hsüan Tsung (shwee-AHND-zoong; ruled 712–56), who ruled China's T'ang (TAHNG) dynasty at the height of its power.

Yang Kuei-fei was said to be one of the only obese women in Chinese history who was also considered a great beauty. She started out as concubine of Hsüan Tsung's son before the emperor decided he wanted her for himself—along with her two sisters. Later she took the general An Lu-shan (703–757) under her wing as her adopted son and (according to palace rumors) lover.

While the emperor, overcome by love for Yang Kuei-fei, neglected his official duties, others struggled for control. Principal among these were Yang's brother and An Lu-shan, who had long been a trusted friend of Hsüan Tsung. T'ang forces suffered a defeat by Arab troops in 751, and An Lu-shan, seeing his chance to take power, launched a rebellion in 755.

Angry palace officials blamed Yang and her brother for the uprising, and pressured Hsüan Tsung to order her execution, which he did. Two years later, An Lu-shan was killed. The tragic story of Yang Kuei-fei would later become a favorite theme among Chinese poets and writers.

she demanded that her name appear before his on official documents, her son rebelled. A power struggle followed, and by 790 Constantine succeeded in taking control. He embarked on a series of unsuccessful wars, however, and became so unpopular that in January 792 he brought Irene back into a position of authority.

This would prove to be a bad decision for Constantine, considering his mother's desire for power, and in January 795, he made another ill-advised move when he left his wife and married one of her ladies-in-waiting. Irene had supported her son in this action, probably because she knew that it would turn many church officials against him—and it did. Realizing that his mother was prepared to remove him, Constantine tried to escape, but he was captured, and on August

15, 797, Irene had him blinded. As a result of this mutilation, he died soon afterward, a result Irene apparently intended.

Conflict over the title "Roman Empire"

Now Irene ruled Byzantium as sole empress, but in so doing, she went too far. Up to that point, she had enjoyed at least a measure of support from the pope. In the West, where few people could read and write, icons were an essential part of worship, and therefore the pope had supported the use of icons. This had effectively made him Irene's ally. On the other hand, the pope was not happy with the idea of a woman controlling Byzantium, and since it was not legal for a woman to rule Byzantium, he could claim that the Roman throne was vacant. Therefore in 800, Pope Leo III crowned Charlemagne "Emperor of the Romans."

Henceforth the term "Roman Empire" would be used to describe the realm ruled by Charlemagne and by later monarchs of the Holy Roman Empire, and the West would never again recognize Byzantium's claim as the true Roman Empire. This was to be one of the most lasting outcomes of Irene's reign, and certainly the most unfortunate from the Byzantine perspective.

At the time, however, the results were not so clear, and Charlemagne sought to strengthen his claim to the title by proposing marriage to Irene. She agreed to the union, recognizing that it would strengthen her hold on power, but she did not remain on the throne long enough to marry Charlemagne.

The end of Irene's reign

A series of misfortunes occurred in the years of Irene's sole rulership, most of them the direct outcome of the confusion that resulted from her seizure of power. Arab forces under Harun al-Rashid (see box in El Cid entry) scored a major victory over the Byzantines, who were forced to pay the Arabs large sums of money. Irene had meanwhile lowered taxes, hoping to win favor from her people, and this further reduced the Byzantine treasury.

In 802, in a revolt led by the Byzantine minister of finance, Irene was overthrown. She escaped to the isle of Lesbos. Despite the many enemies she had made, Irene had many supporters as well, and they continued to support her during the final year of her life. She died in 803 and was later declared a saint in the Greek Orthodox Church.

For More Information

Books

Corrick, James A. *The Byzantine Empire*. San Diego, CA: Lucent Books, 1997.

Durant, Will. *The Age of Faith*. New York: Simon and Schuster, 1950.

Encyclopedia of World Biography, second edition. Detroit: Gale, 1998.

Historic World Leaders. Detroit: Gale, 1994.

Millar, Heather. *China's Tang Dynasty*. New York: Benchmark Books, 1996.

Uglow, Jennifer S., editor. *The Continuum Dictionary of Women's Biography*. New York: Continuum Publishing, 1989.

Women's Firsts. Detroit: Gale, 1997.

Web Sites

"Ancient China: The T'ang, 618–970." [Online] Available http:// www.wsu.edu:8080/~dee/CHEMPIRE/TANG.HTM (last accessed July 26, 2000).

Index

T'ai Tsung *2:* **335–42**, 335 (ill.),
     357, 359, 372
Talas *2:* 342
Tale of Genji 2: 265, 268–71
Tale of the Rose 1: 73
Talmud *2:* 224, 226, 352, 353
Tamerlane *1:* 10, 13, 97, *2:* 278,
     343–48, 343 (ill.)
Tamils *1:* 10
Tancred *2:* 324, 325
T'ang dynasty *1:* 4, *2:* 220, 335,
     336, 338, 341, 357, 360, 361,
     374, 375
Tangier *1:* 157, *2:* 302
Taoism *1:* 4
Tara *2:* 293, 294
Targutai *1:* 130
Tatars *1:* 130, 132
Tauresium *2:* 200
Tebaldo Visconti. *See* Gregory X
     (pope)
Technology *2:* 240–42, 252, 337
Templars *1:* 51
Temujin *1:* 129–31
Tenchi *2:* 341
Tenochtitlán *2:* 252, 253
Terrorists *2:* 316
Teutonic Knights *1:* 15, 19
Texcoco *2:* 252
Thailand *2:* 285, 301
Theobald *1:* 116
Theodora *2:* 199–202, 202 (ill.),
     204–07
Theodoric *1:* 55, 56, 58, 58 (ill.)
Theology *1:* 59, 163, *2:* 351
Theophano *1:* 171, 172
Third Crusade *1:* 108, 111, 173, *2:*
     313, 315, 317, 321
Thomas Aquinas *1:* 117, *2:*
     349–55, 349 (ill.)
Thorfinn *2:* 220
Thoros *2:* 325
Thorstein *2:* 220
Thorvald *2:* 219, 220
Thousand and One Nights, The 1:
     103
Thuringia *1:* 170, 174
Tibet *2:* 214, 300, 301, 303
Timbuktu *2:* 232, 243, 245, 248
Timur Lenk. *See* Tamerlane
Tlacaelel *2:* 254
Toghril Beg *2:* 275, 329, 331
Toghrul *1:* 131–33

Toledo *1:* 35, 36, 101
Tolstoy, Leo *2:* 269
Tomislav *2:* 274
Topa *2:* 286, 287
Torah *2:* 223, 225, 226, 228
Tours *1:* 77, 80
Trabzon *2:* 301
Transylvania *1:* 19, *2:* 346
Travel *1:* 86, 116, 126, *2:* 218,
     220, 286, 297, 301
Travels of Ibn Battuta 2: 303
Treasure of the City of Ladies, The
     1: 74
Treaty of Verdun *1:* 66, *2:* 246
Treaty of Winchester *1:* 109
Trigonometry *2:* 237
Trinity *1:* 2, 6, *2:* 311
Tripoli *2:* 325
Trojan War *1:* 119
Troylus and Criseyde 1: 119
Tu Fu *1:* 4
Tunisia *1:* 24, 25
Turkey *1:* 86, 134, 158, 166, 174,
     187, *2:* 200, 206, 220, 273,
     279, 292, 302, 322, 329, 331,
     333, 343, 345–47. *See also*
     Anatolia; Asia Minor
Turks *1:* 11, 16, 39, 44, 94, 158,
     166, 181, *2:* 273–76, 278,
     279, 321, 322, 324, 336, 340,
     343, 344, 346, 359
Tuscany *1:* 148–50, 180
Twain, Mark *1:* 80
Tyler, Wat *2:* 361, 362

U

Ujjain *2:* 236
Ukraine *1:* 15
Umayyad *1:* 32
Unam Sanctum 1: 141
United States *2:* 229, 231, 235,
     251, 258, 332
United States Declaration of Inde-
     pendence *1:* 109
University of Bologna *1:* 69, 181
University of Cracow *1:* 19
University of Paris *2:* 239, 350,
     351
Upon the Circumstances Which
     Turn the Head of Most Men

Z